Go ahead and put these practical gu... smile at the miracle of wonderful tr... ADHD, and especially in your child. Thank you, Dr. Honos-Webb, for your gift to what ADHD can be.

—Alvin R. Mahrer, Ph.D., professor emeritus of ... nada, ...ntial

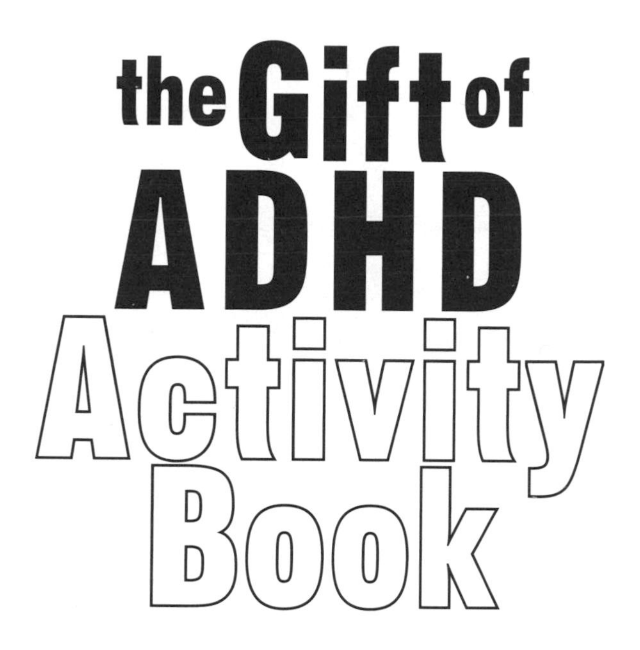

101 Ways to Turn Your Child's Problems into Strengths

LARA HONOS-WEBB, PH.D.

New Harbinger Publications, Inc.

Publisher's Note

This publication is designed to provide accurate and authoritative information in regard to the subject matter covered. It is sold with the understanding that the publisher is not engaged in rendering psychological, financial, legal, or other professional services. If expert assistance or counseling is needed, the services of a competent professional should be sought.

Distributed in Canada by Raincoast Books

New Harbinger Publications, Inc.
5674 Shattuck Avenue
Oakland, CA 94609
www.newharbinger.com

Cover and text design by Amy Shoup; Acquired by Tesilya Hanauer;
Edited by Carole Honeychurch

Printed in the United States of America

Library of Congress Cataloging-in-Publication Data

Honos-Webb, Lara.
The gift of ADHD activity book : 101 ways to turn your child's problems into strengths / Lara Honos-Webb.
p. cm.
ISBN-13: 978-1-57224-515-0 (pbk. : alk. paper)
ISBN-10: 1-57224-515-8 (pbk. : alk. paper)
1. Attention-deficit hyperactivity disorder--Popular works. I. Title.
RJ506.H9H658 2007
618.92'8589--dc22
2007041247

09 08 07

10 9 8 7 6 5 4 3 2 1

First printing

This book is dedicated to Ken, Kenny, and Audrey Webb for giving me the gift of waking up happy every day.

Contents

Acknowledgments

I can't find the words to express the love and gratitude from the depths of my heart to Karen, John, Ed, Chrissty, Grace, and Catherine Honos for their love and support. Thanks to Carole and Bill Webb, Anna, Rosanna, and Dale Chalfant for their constant encouraging presence and occasional babysitting. Thanks to Bill Webb for creating the design of the bingo cards in the book.

I'd like to thank all the same folks and mentors I acknowledged in the first book with New Harbinger Publications, *The Gift of ADHD*, especially Tesilya Hanauer, Melissa Kirk, Heather Mitchener, Lorna Garano, Troy DuFrene, and Earlita Chenault, who I appreciate more and more with each book. I'm grateful to Carole Honeychurch for her masterful edits and making me look good.

Thanks to my mom-buddies and their husbands and children for nourishing my family and soul. I can't express in words my admiration for how hard you work for so little recognition, and my devotion to you for the much-needed and never-frequent-enough moms' nights out. Thanks to Rose Pacini, Jeannie Lopez, Wendy Whittles, Lisa Cloven, Margareth Click, Kiran Berrien Lawrence, Jen Chaney, Tiffany Welker, Sharon Beernink, Neetu Machaiah, and Christine Lydkis.

Thanks to Marc Celentana, Cy Estonactac, and Jenny Yeaggy for fond memories of must-see TV and other adventures.

I will be eternally grateful to Dick and Alison Jones and their family for their remarkable generosity of spirit. Without the lifelong support of John Thomas, I could never have made so many of my dreams come true. Thanks to Kira Mann, lifelong friend and now hipster party buddy, for reaching out to me with all your support over the last few years. I'm grateful to everyone at the Detroit Country Day School, for the lifelong support network. You have provided me with a launching pad that made everything else that came after refreshingly easy in comparison (with the possible exception of childbirth).

I'd like to thank Kelly Howell for her friendship, support, and breakthrough healing technologies. I'm forever grateful to Carol Adrienne for her coaching and continued support. Thanks to Dr. Al Mahrer for being an inspiration and just the revolutionary the world needs now. Thanks to Deborah Harper for inviting me into the world of podcasting.

Thanks to Kim McCoy for being a kindred spirit, to Stephanie Vlahov for climbing the Mt. Everest of you-know-what, and to Renie Oxley for reminding me that to get to the next level I have to speak to my truth—it worked!

Thanks to all of my clients for sharing your mystery with me. You are my primary inspiration.

To the most important people in the world: Molly McCann and Nino Kakulia for their loving care of Kenny and Audrey.

Introduction

The 101 activities presented in this book are based on the change in worldview I put forth in my first book, *The Gift of ADHD: How to Transform Your Child's Problems into Strengths* (2005). That change in worldview can simply be described as focusing on the gifts and strengths that children with attention-deficit/hyperactivity disorder (ADHD) have in abundance. The shift is much more radical than simply finding strengths because it's about actually seeing ADHD as a gift. The very same behaviors, traits, and expressions that get labeled as symptoms can, through a different lens, be seen as strengths that have an important contribution to make to our communities and culture.

GETTING WHAT YOU FOCUS ON

Even if you find yourself doubtful about the premise that ADHD can be seen as a gift, there is little doubt that adopting such a belief would help transform your child's problems into strengths. Any serious student of human behavior will agree that whatever you focus on in your life, you will get more of. Research on *optimistic explanatory styles*—taking credit for good behavior and outcomes while looking for environmental causes of bad behavior and outcomes—has shown that finding benefits and focusing on them will increase mental and physical health and can even increase the length of life (Giltay et al. 2006). So this is no Pollyanna fancy; rather, it is serious science affecting life and health.

With this simple principle in mind—in life, you get more of what you focus on—you can make dramatic changes in the life of your ADHD child with some simple activities that apply this principle. It breaks my heart to think of what can happen to a child when you focus primarily on perceived deficits and disorders. Imagine the dramatic transformations you could see when you withdraw your focus on these weaknesses. Now think of how this change will accelerate when you intensify your awareness and attention on the strengths of your child. We will examine this dynamic more closely and learn skills to bring it to the fore later in the book.

WHAT IS ADHD?

ADHD can be broken down into three main clusters or deficits. The first cluster is *inattention*—the inability to know what task to attend to or not being able to stay focused long enough to finish a task. This usually shows up as poor school performance, forgotten homework or chores, and difficulty getting organized. A second cluster is *impulsivity*, which means your child has difficulty controlling urges and often speaks out in irreverent ways. An example of impulsivity is when your child interrupts others and can't wait her own turn. The last cluster is *hyperactivity*, indicated by excess physical or mental restlessness. Your child may seem as if she is driven by a motor, may squirm more than others, and may not be able to sit in her chair at school.

Many of these same symptoms can be caused by depression, anxiety, or major stressors. To be sure your child really has ADHD, these other possible causes should be ruled out first.

WHAT'S RIGHT WITH A CHILD WITH ADHD?

The quickest way to transform your child's problem into strengths is to ask yourself repeatedly, "What is right with my child?" This will prompt you to find your child's gifts. One parent, troubled that her child didn't do as well in school as other children, began to look for her child's strengths. With some practice, this parent was struck by her son's creative and artistic talents and began to actively foster those qualities. When she fell back into comparing her son with other kids his age who seemed to easily excel in school, she asked herself, "What's right with my child?" This way, she could get back on the path of encouraging her child's gifts and moving in a positive direction.

It's normal to compare your child to others. There is no way to avoid doing so in our competitive culture. I think that there is no freedom from worry when you are a parent, but you can find freedom *in* your worry. That means that you recognize that worry is the work of being a parent, and you channel that anxious energy into productive action and stay positive.

For example, if you are worried about your child's school performance, take action by talking with her teachers, helping her with her homework, and getting access to other resources (occupational therapy, speech therapy) that might increase her chances of adapting to school. Sometimes a diagnosis of ADHD opens the door to resources like occupational therapy and more one-on-one attention. Take advantage of these resources while keeping in mind that you need to find your child's real gifts and focus on those.

By focusing on your child's strengths, you pay extra attention to what she does right and find many ways to channel those gifts. This might feel frustrating if you hold on to old expectations you've held for your child. For example, if you cherished the idea of your child as a great scholar and it turns out her gifts are in the artistic arena, you will have to adjust your expectations. Try to remember that your child will excel at what she loves, and that a passion in any arena can fuel building skills in other arenas.

One of the main reasons to focus on gifts is that doing so can become a self-fulfilling prophecy. Children often live up to (or "down to") our expectations. If we focus on what our children do well, they will continue to excel and build skills and passion. If you focus on what she cannot do, your child may adapt a style of patching up weaknesses and always feeling less than others. By demanding good results in those areas where your child doesn't excel, you are in effect focusing on those weaknesses. You will likely get more of what you focus on—in this case, more poor performance. In addition, there are drawbacks for the child who puts enormous pressure on herself to succeed in school at all costs.

THE PRICE OF BEING A COMPETITIVE KNOW-IT-ALL

In our current cultural climate, kids are led to believe that showing how much they know is the only way to demonstrate their worth. But this emphasis on learning for the sake of feeling superior to others can lead to deep trouble. As a psychologist, I see that the people who are driven by the need to show how smart they are can be crippled when it comes to discovering their true gifts. If you are driven by the motive to be better than others at any cost, you will be forced to invest most of your time and energy into overlearning and overpreparing. That means you will spend enormous amounts of time, even after you have understood the material, memorizing it so you can regurgitate it on cue. The time you spend overlearning is time you can't use to explore the world. You may have a very specialized and unique gift in an arena that you never discover because your time is consumed with mastery in arenas that are not truly where your greatest natural gifts are.

FIVE GIFTS OF ADHD

When you begin to focus on your child's gifts, you will discover many unique and spectacular things about her. In *The Gift of ADHD* (2005), I outline five different gifts that I've observed in clients and students who have been diagnosed with ADHD. In the young people I've worked with, I've found that ADHD is usually accompanied by great creativity, exuberance, emotional sensitivity, interpersonal intuition, and increased ecological consciousness. Your child may have all of these, as well as other gifts. While we examine the common strengths I've just mentioned, don't forget to continue looking for additional gifts your child may possess.

The Gift of Creativity

Most ADHD children demonstrate gifts in creativity, whether through drawing, a different way of seeing the world, or some other form of artistic expression. Some people who have worked with ADHD kids for decades have said that they actually doubt the ADHD diagnosis if they don't see evidence of artistic creativity.

Some parents are tempted to dismiss the creative gifts because they fear they are not practical and won't lead to career success later in life. If you share this view, remind yourself that despite our culture's sometimes narrow definition of success, many fields demand creativity, and there are many ways to be very successful in artistic fields. The world needs creative artists. In addition, many have argued that we are evolving toward an economy where the creative individuals will be the most successful, as other jobs are being outsourced. Cutting-edge innovation seems to be driving the economy more and more. Nurture and nourish this precious gift in your child and try to open your mind to alternate forms of success.

The Gift of Exuberance

Try to view your child's "hyperactivity" as exuberance. Entertain the idea that her high energy and even wildness can be an incredible resource. If you can find ways to channel this energy, your child will be able to accomplish anything.

The Gift of Emotional Sensitivity

What can look like uncontrollable outbursts in ADHD children can often be directly traced to another gift—emotional sensitivity. Your child's behavior is more extreme than other children because your child feels more deeply. This depth of feeling and heightened awareness can be a great gift in life. If you can train, coach, or teach your child to name her emotions and tolerate them, she can become an emotional genius. Recent developments in psychology have shown that emotional intelligence is more predictive of lifelong success than even traditional measures of IQ (Shapiro 1997).

The Gift of Interpersonal Intuition

What is often characterized as poor social judgment can alternately be seen as what we call *interpersonal intuition*. This means that your ADHD child is often intuiting and acting out unexpressed emotions or conflicts in her environment. This interpersonal intuition, the ability to read others like a book, can be torture for the school-age child dealing with the immaturity and bullying that is standard practice at these ages. But the ability to intuit unspoken emotional situations can help her navigate complex situations as an adult, especially if your child can learn to deal with this kind of emotional input early.

Some of the healing play activities in this book will help your child gain some distance from being flooded by these experiences. Some of the activities are designed to increase your own sense of play and whimsy and can help turn around your child's experience.

The Gift of Ecological Consciousness

An emblematic image of an ADHD child is a kid sitting at their school desk idly staring out the window. This "negligent" behavior may be driven by another gift—that of ecological consciousness. This means that ADHD kids feel especially connected to the natural and organic world. While your child may feel the natural world, the great outdoors, is teeming with life, she may feel stifled when stuck indoors for most of the day. Ecological consciousness is one gift that is desperately needed in our culture. When nurtured, it blooms into an instinct toward preservation of natural lands, water sources, and animal life.

FROM PATCHING UP WEAKNESSES TO BUILDING STRENGTHS

The main shift in thinking found in *The Gift of ADHD* and this book is this: move your focus from patching up weaknesses to identifying and building strengths. This means that if your child has difficulty with spelling but is excellent at problem solving and generating new ideas, you should spend most of your time and attention giving her complex problems to solve and helping her apply her creative ideas. You try to find ways to get her to gain essential skills without focusing on what does not come easily or well for her.

This doesn't mean that you make no effort to build skills in arenas that don't come easily. It just means that most of your time and attention will be better spent building on existing strengths and passions.

The Kellers and the Johnsons

The Kellers were desperately and excessively worried about their son John's poor social skills. John may have had poor social skills, but he was academically brilliant, reading books voraciously much above his grade level. However, the family paid no attention to this remarkable gift. They hardly noticed the thick science-fiction books he carried with him everywhere. One time he even got in trouble at school for reading a Kurt Vonnegut book during math class. John's parents' energy was entirely focused on patching up the child's social deficits, meaning they missed out on fostering his gift for literature.

The Johnsons worried endlessly about their daughter Jane's mediocre performance in school. Although Jane did poorly academically, she was very easygoing and quite popular with her peers. Not only did she have many friends, but she was kind and sensitive toward the kids who were picked on. The popular kids invited her to many social events at the same time that many of the kids who were struggling socially turned to her for support and encouragement. She managed the painful hierarchy that is common in school by using her social status to include those kids who were in pain.

Neither family looked for or acknowledged the substantial gifts each child already had. Can you imagine how the lives of these families might be different if they recognized and spent most of their time and energy on their child's gifts? What if the Kellers were thrilled and excited about John's avid interest in books? What if they fed his passion and imagined him growing up to be an author, a teacher, or a publisher? How do you think each child and family would feel if they changed their focus? Imagine if the Johnsons focused most of their time and energy on celebrating the social ease that Jane showed without any effort or struggle. They could spend their time imagining the future of a woman who could facilitate social connections and succeed at almost anything with her ability to connect with others.

Differences Are Not Disorders

One of the central themes of *The Gift of ADHD* was that differences do not make disorders. In the stories above you may have thought for yourself that John could easily grow up to be someone like a Bill Gates or an eccentric author whose surplus of creative and intellectual gifts simply overshadows the necessity of developing strong social ties. With Jane, it's easy to think of her social ease and charm in someone like an Oprah or other media star who connects powerfully with others but doesn't necessarily need to excel in academic skills.

When one takes a larger perspective and thinks of all the billions of people on the earth and the radically different cultures we come from in addition to the different values, skills, and interests we all hold, it seems remarkable that anyone can ever get along with another person at all. With so much diversity, coupled with a shift in perspective that celebrates differences, the force toward normalizing our children to all be academic high achievers in a narrow band of domains seems unrealistic. There are four ways to shift your perspective to see that differences are not disorders:

1. **Reframe.** Seen from a different perspective, what appears to be a deficit can be reframed as a positive trait. In *The Gift of ADHD*, I reframe spaciness as creativity, hyperactivity as exuberance, emotional outbursts as intense sensitivity, and social complications as interpersonal intuition. So many differences

can be reframed or understood as being gifts in and of themselves.

2. **Assess Your Child's Strengths and Weaknesses.** Each person is a unique combination of strengths, weaknesses, skills, and interests. Someone with an outstanding gift will often have weaknesses that match. In some ways, it's just a matter of having only so much time and energy in one's day and life. If you are brilliant intellectually and passionate about reading, you simply won't have the motivation, time, or energy to develop all other arenas of competence.

   Recent theories of intelligence agree that there are many types of intelligence, including mathematical, verbal, musical, athletic, interpersonal, emotional, and spiritual intelligence, among many others (Gardner 1999). Many times, deciding that something is a disorder may simply be overlooking the existing strengths and focusing obsessively on weaknesses that are predictable when you examine a child's level of functioning across many different arenas. A striking example of this is Lance Armstrong's experience. Armstrong's mother has said that he could have been a poster child for ADHD when he was a child. He was very active and not a highly motivated student. When one looks at what he has accomplished and who he has become, it is clear he did not have a disorder—he was simply built to do great things in the arena of sports and to serve as an exceptional model of strength, fortitude, and persistence in the face of a devastating health crisis.

3. **Note Developmental Spurts and Lags.** Each person develops at his or her own pace. And once we recognize that there are multiple arenas for development—including intellectual, emotional, motor, and interpersonal—it again seems predictable that each child would make leaps in one arena while other areas might naturally lag behind.

   Many parents believe that boys develop motor skills before language whereas girls develop language skills and lag behind on motor development. As you expand your understanding of the wide arena of development, try to consider all the possibilities at play when your child develops more quickly in one area than another. For example, it's easy to imagine a child who is working toward expressing his social skills and motor skills while lagging behind on intellectual skills, or vice versa. In addition, it would be predictable that if a child had to cope with any stressor—including a family crisis, a health crisis, or even just changing schools or grades—that any one of these developmental tasks could be put on hold while the child simply coped with the change he or she was facing.

   Sometimes what looks like a disorder is a failure of patience. I have had clients who came in to my office with intense worry and concern about their child and who felt pressured by teachers or pediatricians to try medications when their child didn't excel in one area or another. In some of these cases, simply waiting a year or two allowed the problem to resolve itself.

4. **Recognize Cultural Expectations.** What looks like a disorder in one cultural setting might just be a difference

in another cultural setting. The failure to take a look from a larger perspective may account for some differences getting labeled as disorders. In some cases I have seen children described as having an academic deficit because their grades were predominantly C's. While in some cases a C grade can represent an impairment, many times it is actually predictably average and does not represent a disorder at all. A diagnosis may result in one setting because the expectations are for academic excellence and average performance is viewed as a serious deficit.

Alternatively, in other cultures there are few or no expectations for academic excellence. In some of these cases, intellectual development lags because there is no cultural or social support for it. In such cases, a broader perspective might view these children as either socially disadvantaged from a mainstream bias or simply raised with different values and skills. To say that the child has a mental disorder, as is implied in the diagnosis of ADHD, seems inappropriate.

LABELS: THE GOOD, THE BAD, AND WHAT YOU CAN DO

In *The Gift of ADHD*, I argue that children who are properly diagnosed are demonstrably different from other children. I don't argue that there is no such thing as ADHD.

In any arena of performance, expectations translate into outcomes. Imagine a loud booming voice in the mind of a developing child who is struggling to forge an identity and understanding of who she is and where she fits in the world. This voice tells her that there is something fundamentally wrong with her. Naturally, this would frighten this child, perhaps causing her (and her caregivers) to begin to look tirelessly at this perceived problem. If a child is focused primarily on what is wrong with her, that very focus can become a self-fulfilling prophecy.

The Good: See Differences, Not Disorder

The good thing about labels is that both parents and children often feel a sense of relief when they see all their differences "hang together" under one name. It makes them feel not so alone and different. It also gives them hope that they can begin to improve in their functioning. The label also allows teachers and others to acknowledge the child's differences and enables them to give the child resources they need and to be responsive to those differences.

In terms of expectations and your interactions with the child, appreciate the differences, but maintain high expectations that realistically reflect the child's gifts and passionate interests. For those who work with people with ADHD, this is sometimes called "taking the difference while leaving the disorder."

Many parents and teachers struggle with how to tell the child about the diagnosis. I recommend using the gifts as a bridge to reframing the label. Both children and parents benefit from having a clear idea about how the needs of the child will differ from others. The best way to explore those differences is to focus on the gifts, translating hyperactivity into exuberance, for example, and to problem solve on how the impairments that result from having more difficulty sitting still can be addressed and solved in the classroom and other settings.

It is also important for the parent, teacher, and child to relate to the label. This means that rather than just accepting the label without question, you should spend some time forging an understanding of what the meaning of the label will be. Parents can ask their child, "What does ADHD mean to you?" You can then listen carefully to the child, correcting any destructive beliefs and addressing concerns. Parents, teachers, and children would do well to remember that research shows that children with ADHD do not have lower intelligence than other children, as measured by IQ scores. On one subscale—the ability to hold information in short-term memory—they tend to do more poorly. But you can see that this one result should not lead to the dramatic reduction in expectations that often follows a diagnosis of ADHD.

What a diagnosis of ADHD should mean for the child, parents, and teachers is an opportunity to explore and recognize the child's differences and respond appropriately to those differences. In short, parents and teachers can be responsive to the label rather than passively accepting it along with its baggage. One simple adjustment parents and teachers can make is to be more concrete and less abstract, for example incorporating project-based learning into the child's education. Also, children with ADHD can be helped along by being given more time for transitions and having their greater need for physical movement respected.

The Bad: Concerns About Labels

There are concerns about the label of ADHD (as with any diagnostic label). However, by being aware of these concerns you can take preventative action so your child won't experience these possible negative consequences.

One concern is that the diagnosis of ADHD will lead to low motivation. For example, a child may interpret the label to mean that they are impaired and have a disease. She might then wonder why she should waste her time on a playing field which she can't win. Pay attention for any signs your child might be saying to herself, "I have a disease—why try?" You can counter this destructive belief with stories of those who overcame great obstacles and also reminders that academic performance is substantially based on persistence and motivation and that there is little to no relationship between ADHD and intellectual abilities.

Another concern about the ADHD label is that it could result in your child developing *low self-efficacy*—a feeling that she cannot control the outcomes of her life or achieve the goals she has set for herself. Efficacy is ultimately about one's ability to control the world, to act on it and make things happen. The risk is that children will hear the label and believe "I'm a victim, I have a disease, and I'm not in control." This can be dangerous because motivation and persistence will be strongly related to your child's belief about her efficacy. A sense of being able to act on the world and make things happen is a basic requirement for any person to put forth the effort to make her dreams come true.

Another concern about the diagnosis is that it will lead to the belief that something is fundamentally wrong with the child. You may want to watch for global or general beliefs, feelings, or statements from your child that she is somehow essentially flawed or will never be good enough. One way to think of it is that these beliefs can become like the "soundtrack" of your child's life—a background belief that affects the entire tone of her life. It can be possible for the child to hear the words "deficit" and "disorder" and feel that the label is adding insult to injury. As a parent, you should be aware of this possibility, taking care to counteract any negative internalizations and to provide your child with positive feedback about who she really is.

What You Can Do: Question Labels

Given some of these concerns about labels, parents may want to question the label before moving forward with a diagnosis. However, by questioning, I don't mean rejecting. Sometimes the diagnosis and the medications to treat ADHD are appropriate. The research indicates that medications are effective in reducing ADHD symptoms. While many parents are aware of the growing concerns about side effects, it remains true that for some children, medication allows them to function much more easily and effectively.

In questioning the label of ADHD, parents may simply want to ensure that a thorough assessment has been conducted before a diagnosis is made. In some cases, children have been given a diagnosis and a prescription for medication based only on a decrease in school performance or motivation. Many of the same symptoms of ADHD can be caused by normal developmental stages, depression, anxiety, or serious stressors. As a parent, you will want to be vigilant and ask how and why those other possibilities have been ruled out.

Another matter for parents to reflect on is the deeper philosophical issues. Do your child's problems rise to the level of a bona fide mental disorder? Is it possible that issues of control, conformity, and compliance are at stake? A child who questions the real-world applications of what they are learning in school may be showing self-reliance rather than defiance. A child who questions the status quo may actually have a good point. Perhaps we are too quick to label a questioning mind as a disordered mind. As an example, I've seen children with ADHD diagnosed primarily on the rejection of homework and the attendant poor performance in school. Interestingly, even scholars of education have recently decried the problems of homework and the toll it takes (Bennett and Kalish 2006). These scholars write about the problem of too much homework taking up the time a child could be spending with family or developing other interests. In addition, there remain questions about the educational value of homework itself. Homework focuses a child on accumulation and demonstration of knowledge rather than real-world applications and experience. In this way, sometimes children who are diagnosed with ADHD are accurately reflecting the failure of the current educational system to keep up with the demands of the digital age. With the advent of search engines like Google, global Internet access, and software technologies to promote novel learning experiences, accumulating and demonstrating knowledge becomes less valuable. Other skills such as adaptability and the ability to think critically and consider contexts become more important in the age of information explosion. The Bill and Melinda Gates Foundation launched an initiative to address the failure of schools that were designed to prepare students for the industrial culture and are not up to speed on the digital age.

At an even more profound level, it's not even clear that we know what it means to pay attention. Few have asked, "What *is* attention?" One of my observations is that people pay attention to what they are interested in, what is intensely meaningful for their life purpose. I think of Lance Armstrong, whose mother reported he had difficulty paying attention in school. Because there are so many possible career choices, gifts, and arenas for excellence and interest, it seems likely that many children perceive that getting good grades simply for the sake of conformity and compliance will not serve their general life course. But it's more obvious what getting good grades means in a class they love. Even children who get diagnosed with ADHD often show good academic performance in classes that truly interest and engage them. Parents may want to pay close attention to where their child does well to determine if the child seems to be preparing for excellence in one arena. Children may realize what many parents are too afraid to see: many people achieve great success in life without having been uniformly good students.

While a child's needs for play, connection, and exploration of the world have remained the same, our culture has accelerated its demands for academic performance and competition. While most adults have been able to keep up with the breakneck pace allowed by modern technologies, it is not healthy or possible for a developing child to do so.

One other point of reflection for parents in their process of questioning the label of ADHD is exploring the role that competitiveness might play in the diagnosis. Of course it's important that you have high expectations for your child, but be wary of letting your own ego get in the way of your child's natural progress. Consider whether your personal need to have your child succeed academically is playing a factor in your expectation of a diagnosis. A diagnosis of ADHD requires that there be an impairment in functioning in two or more settings in addition to the presence of the symptoms of hyperactivity, impulsiveness, and difficulty concentrating. All kids have some of those symptoms some of the time. The diagnosis is intended to reflect a serious impairment. A child whose academic performance is simply average may therefore not reflect an impairment in functioning. For example, a child who is artistic may excel at design and other related talents but just scrape by in more academic courses. If parents can stay centered and take a broader perspective—assuming that the child will be a great success in the design field or an artistic career—the child's performance may seem less like a symptom of a disorder and more like a reflection of his or her true abilities and interests.

FIVE NEW PARADIGM SHIFTS

In applying the simple principle of finding and focusing on strengths in my work with parents, children, and teachers, I realized that there were five additional fundamental changes in worldview that were required to give ADHD kids the edge they need. This book will review the five additional paradigm shifts I have developed or elaborated on since *The Gift of ADHD* was released and provide concrete examples of specific activities that will foster these changes. The five shifts in worldview that parents can effect to set in motion a positive interaction cycle are the following:

- Learn coaching skills
- Cultivate your child's emotional intelligence
- Stand up for your child's strengths
- See the world through your child's eyes
- Exercise flexible thinking

In chapter 1, you will learn how thinking of yourself as a coach can transform your relationship with your child. Once you see that much of what you need to teach your child is *procedural learning* (skills that require practice and repetition), much like learning to ride a bike, you will realize that you don't have to rely only on discipline and consequences to get behavioral change. In chapter 2, you will learn how validating your child's emotions and helping her become easily able to label all of her emotions without punishment can get rid of a lot of what gets called bad behavior. Many times, misbehavior is just mad behavior or sad behavior or scared behavior. In chapter 3, you will have fun with becoming your child's advocate and translating his behavior for teachers, peers, and parents in a positive way.

You want your child to feel like she lives in a friendly world, and you can help make that happen. Chapter 4 guides you in respecting your child's differences. Many times what appears to be defiance is simply a matter of a child honoring her own inner imagination or compelling sense of urgency. You will learn to cultivate those areas of deep passion in your child while minimizing family disruptions. Chapter 5 will help you and your child understand the world in more complex ways. You will learn that you can maintain high standards while letting go of the competitiveness that is driven by comparison with others. You can learn to honor your child's gifts while helping her succeed in school. In addition to these paradigm shifts, the five numbered chapters will contain specific activities you can do that will be great fun for you and your child.

ABOUT THE ACTIVITIES

The activities in the book are based on the five paradigm shifts. They will nurture and nourish emotional intelligence, social intelligence, physical activity in some cases, and fun in all cases. Browse through some of the activities and find one that seems like fun to you. It will help transform your child's problems into strengths. Many of the activities are designed with your busy lifestyle in mind. For example, some of the activities you can do in the car while driving.

The activities are designed to be fun for the parent *and* child. This is not like other activity books that focus on building your child's brain and that come with implicit performance demands. The exercises will help empower your child. They usually contain within them the seeds of positive suggestion and give her the experience of control over her environment. These exercises can help you and your family open up to joy and learn how to play in our overscheduled, stressed-out world. Some of the benefits you can expect include: 1) creating new patterns of interacting and connecting with your child, 2) channeling energy in ways that increase emotional intelligence and social intelligence, and 3) validating your child's perspective and thereby creating a happier, more effective family.

1

Learn Coaching Skills

Parents of ADHD kids are frustrated. They are frustrated with their kids. They're frustrated that their child does not follow directions and that he is so energetic it seems impossible to keep up with him. They're frustrated with teachers who don't seem to have the resources to give their child the individual attention that's so necessary. They're frustrated with themselves for not having the energy and patience to keep up with him and make him just like everybody else.

A major source of this frustration is that parents blame themselves for their child's problems, including school performance, social rejection or exclusion, behavioral problems, and emotional outbursts. When a child fails, the parent internalizes the failure, feeling like they are fundamentally flawed as parents.

One simple shift in perspective can turn all this around.

THE PARENT AS COACH

Think of your role in parenting as being like that of a coach. A coach doesn't hide in shame when she sees a player miss a shot or goal. A coach thinks of her job as building skills and solving problems. A coach realizes that for a player to perform well, he needs to practice, practice, practice. She knows that sometimes a simple change in technique can improve performance. A coach knows that in order for a child to reach some developmental levels, she will need to repeat herself over and over again. A coach doesn't resent the need for repetition but understands it as an essential ingredient in building skills. I remember when I was training as a figure skater and every single time I had a coaching session, I was reminded many times, "Keep your weight on the ball of your foot." The coach didn't get frustrated that she had to repeat this every single time she met with me. She didn't feel the need to punish me when I didn't conform to perfect technique. It's probably the same as being reminded to bend your knees when skiing or to change hand positioning when golfing or playing tennis.

In a similar way, you may need to say every day, multiple times to your child, "Talk in your normal voice" when he is whining or "Talk it through" when he starts to act out his anger. Coaches don't punish the person in training for not executing techniques correctly. A coach understands that repetition of feedback is necessary to take the trainee to the next level. The coach also understands that when the trainee does make a developmental leap, there will be yet another stylistic or technical element that will need constant repetition.

Also, notice that the coach calmly and clearly states to the player what he needs to do. The coach does not yell about what the person needs to stop doing. For example, the coach doesn't scream in frustration, "Stop straightening your legs!" This strategy doesn't work because it doesn't tell the player what he *should* do. It doesn't solve a problem; it chides, and depending on tone, may even humiliate.

The other thing is that you get what you aim for. You increase what you focus on. If you put your attention on straight legs, even if you're saying don't do it, you will likely get more straight legs. Think how much more effective it would be to use consistent, gentle reminders to the player to bend his legs.

DON'T AFFIX BLAME, FIX THE PROBLEM

A coach knows that even with constant repetition, if problems persist, then they need to do some problem solving. Rather than blaming herself or the player for not following directions, she sets out to discover why that player is unable to follow the guidance given.

I remember in my own clinical training, I had a supervisor who advised me to set stricter limits with a particular client. I consistently had a difficult time doing what she recommended. I felt bad but couldn't identify why I was struggling so much with this particular client and issue. Fortunately, my supervisor took the approach of figuring out why I was struggling rather than punishing me for not complying. She identified that I thought I was being mean to the client by setting the boundaries that were needed. As soon as my supervisor realized this, she was able to give me information that corrected my misunderstanding. She convincingly showed me that what the client desperately needed and wanted was someone who could keep firm boundaries with her, helping her to feel contained. This was what the client needed, and giving it to her wasn't being mean to her. This information and the resulting change in perspective helped me to follow through and set appropriate limits. I needed the information that for some clients, strict limit setting can be what they are desperately searching for.

In this example, the coach (my supervisor) had to bridge the gap between her understanding of the technique and my lack of experience. It required her to adopt a problem-solving attitude and to try to see the struggle from my perspective. She had to get inside my mind. She had to see that I didn't have her rich clinical experience, and that at that time I lacked knowledge of this particular type of client. She had to see the issue from my perspective in order to see my error in thinking.

I have become convinced that most of the bad behavior of ADHD children can be solved by the same strategy:

1. Identifying the problem, such as, "My child does not follow directions"
2. Adopting a problem-solving attitude, not a blaming one
3. Avoiding the urge to punish
4. Making a serious effort to get inside the mind of your child
5. Asking yourself and your child why the behavior makes sense
6. Correcting any misperceptions and providing information that will solve the problem

I have met many wonderful parents and educators who have adopted this attitude and found to their great delight that on some occasions, the child's refusal to follow directions was because he had a better solution or strategy! Be open to the possibility that there is a method to your child's "madness."

EMPHASIZE PROCEDURAL LEARNING, NOT CONSEQUENCES

Procedural learning (learning a skill that requires practice, like riding a bike) means that I assume that you don't know how to accomplish a certain task, so I provide you with the resources, training, information, and modeling that you will need to learn the new skill. If you were trying to teach your child to ride a bike, you wouldn't put him in time-out each time he fell. You would show him what he needed to do differently, while providing emotional support and motivation to keep going. This approach can be applied to teaching your child appropriate behaviors, emotional intelligence, and social skills. Instead of frustration for the parent and consequences for the child, the parent learns to implement the following elements of procedural learning:

- Give information
- Build skills
- Problem solve
- Use repetition
- Motivate and persist

Although this will require more from you than simple consequences for bad behavior, you can consider it a long-term investment in the health and happiness of you and your child. While consequences work in the short term, they don't teach the required skills your child needs to succeed in many different environments. Once your child learns the basic approach of gathering information, building skills, problem solving, and practicing, he can apply these to school, sports, and friendships and maintain high levels of motivation and persistence.

ACTIVITIES

The activities in this section will help you act as your child's coach. All of the activities can be done with resources that you will likely have on hand. Set time aside to do at least one activity a day. These activities can be fun and will help you and your child focus on strengths rather than weaknesses.

1. The Hearty WHOOPS!

One of the most important things a coach can do is to motivate his child to keep going even when the child goofs up. You can practice this by having your child make silly mistakes and practicing an exaggerated "whoops!" response. Imagine a clown who slips on a banana peel. He or she most likely exaggerates the fall, making dramatic gestures and silly faces to amplify the stupid mistake. You want your child to be able to have a healthy wince and admit mistakes but not be stopped by them. Don't waste your time trying to teach your child to be perfect. Don't try to teach your child not to fail. Teach your child the healthy rebound—resilience. Every life will face disappointment, rejection, failure. You don't want to teach your child to be failure phobic. Play at failing and making a quick recovery. This way, your child won't be tempted to hold only small dreams to avoid failure. He also won't be stopped when he does encounter failure. This is the key recipe for success—big dreams plus not being stopped by rejection, disappointment, and failure.

You can do this activity by taking turns with your child, practicing a pratfall—like a clown actually falling down on the floor. You can also practice it by spilling water or carrying a load of laundry and dropping it all. You can also practice it in real-life situations, including when your child brings home a quiz with a mistake or makes a bad play in a sporting event. This activity will take some pressure off of your child while bonding you and your child together as you show your own potential for silliness. Have fun trying to outdo each other with your hearty whoops!

2. The Magic Can

The most important skill you can help your child to build is the ability to tame his messes. A central problem associated with ADHD that hurts success in relationships and professional settings is disorganization. Most parents complain that their children don't like to clean their rooms, but ADHD kids take this to a whole new level. By remembering that you can approach their profound disorganization with persistence, advice, and repeated reminders as a coach would, you will get more success than by punishing your child for not following directions to maintain an organized life. You can coach your child toward gaining the basic skills in a playful way that will go much farther than threatening consequences or nagging. The creativity of ADHD children gives them a huge tolerance for big messes.

Your child will need constant, gentle reinforcement on a daily basis to ingrain lifelong habits. Organization will most likely always be a weak spot, so have patience.

You can develop basic skills for organization with a fun game called The Magic Can. You and your family can create an enchanted receptacle out of a trash can. This can will be just for the child and can be designed to remind him of his favorite magical stories or characters—Harry Potter, the Jedi from *Star Wars*, or whatever engages him. Decorate the can with paint, photos, and sparkles to make it evocative of magic and their favorite wizard or character. Explain to your child that he increases his magic powers by trusting in "the force." He demonstrates this trust by throwing out unneeded papers, broken toys, or other things he no longer needs. Teach him to throw out five things every single day into the magic can. Each time he throws something out, he is to declare, "Let the force be with me," "I clear the way for my magic powers," or some other phrase or affirmation that empowers him and demonstrates the benefits of clearing out his messes.

In addition to a garbage can, you can create variations on the principle of clearing way for the force with a dirty clothes hamper, a toy storage bin, or a bookshelf, among endless possibilities. The point is to reinforce, on a daily basis, small steps toward organization. If your child is younger and more into monsters, dragons, or dinosaurs, you can decorate the bins or garbage cans as a monster and tell him that he has to keep the monster tame by feeding it every day.

3. Reality Show

One of the biggest tools coaches in the real world use is video. They tape a player's performance and let him watch himself in action. If you have a video camera or a regular camera or can borrow one, you can offer your child this high-level coaching technique. Reality shows are all the rage, and the kids will love the idea of creating your own family reality show. Pick one day as "reality show day" and have one person take photos or videotape as much candid interaction as possible. You can also take a lead from the shows like *Supernanny* and *Nanny 911* and ask a friend or family member to come into your family to observe and share observations with family members. You might also choose a problematic behavior of your ADHD child and, like a producer of a reality show, egg your child on to display the bad behavior for the camera or in front of the "supernanny."

Once you have created a reality show—a videotape, a collection of photos, or the observations of another person—plan a time to watch the reality show with the whole family. Watch it together and discuss what you see. If you invited an observer to join in the fun, let them share their observations while the family listens. It's amazing what an impact seeing himself on camera can have on your child, making him aware of what his behavior looks like from the outside or how huge his messes have become. The whole family can act as a coach and see what people could do better to connect more, appreciate each other more, and celebrate each other's differences. In addition to correcting bad behaviors, you should focus more on increasing your family's harmony and getting a good laugh out of each other's foibles and eccentricities.

4. Can I Do It? Yes, I Can.

Bob the Builder, a popular TV and book character for younger kids, has a favorite slogan he uses when faced with a building job that runs into trouble. He shouts out to his crew, "Can we fix it?" and the crew shouts back, "Yes we can!" This activity is inspired by Bob the Builder and world-famous life coach Anthony Robbins, who developed the term "CANI," to mean Constant And Never-ending Improvement (1991). You can teach your child a variation on these inspirations by letting him know that when he comes up against a challenge or problem, whether it's homework, sports, or relationships, he can say, "CANI do it? Yes, I can!" This simple phrase can help him to remember that not only can he plow ahead with confidence, but that he should aim for constant and never-ending improvement.

When you are with your child, you can capture the enthusiasm of Bob the Builder and shout out with full expression, "CANI do it? Yes, I can!" You can model for your child this ability to direct exuberance toward solving problems. When your child is tempted to say "I can't" or "I won't," remind him what "CANI do it?" stands for. When your child is disappointed because someone else is doing better, remind him that the goal is his own constant and never-ending improvement, and it has nothing to do with comparing himself to other kids. You can also ask your child questions like:

- If you were to get better and better and better, what would you be like?
- How could you do this better?

5. Driving Activity: Roving Reporter

Many approaches to ADHD define the child's inability to follow directions as an inherent deficit caused by brain pathology. However, if you think of following directions as a procedural skill that you can help your child acquire, you can coach your child to great improvements. ADHD kids often don't follow directions because: 1) they don't understand the directions clearly, 2) they didn't know the timeline for the task and planned to do it later, or 3) they weren't motivated to do it. This exercise will teach your child skills for resolving these problems.

Choose a time when you're driving with your child in the car. When you have a few minutes to talk, ask him to play a game with you called Roving Reporter. In this game, he gets to ask questions he is interested in, pretending that he's an investigative reporter trying to get the best answer possible. Tell your child that a good reporter has to ask the basic questions of who, what, where, why, and when. One of the huge gifts of ADHD children is their insatiable curiosity, so he will likely have many arenas for investigation. He might ask, "What's the funniest thing that ever happened to you?" or "What's the best meal you ever had?" or millions of other possibilities. You can encourage your child to interview as many people as possible and remind your child of the importance of the five basic "W" questions. You can use follow-up drive time to ask for a report on the question currently under investigation. Not only are you exposing your child to a possible career choice, but you're giving him a simple skill set for pursuing his intense curiosity. Once you teach your child this skill in a fun way, linked to his own questions, you can remind him at opportune moments to apply this strategy at home and at school when given directions. The answer to the "why" question will give him motivation, the answer to the "when" question will ensure he is aware of time constraints, and the answers to the "who," "what," and "where" questions will increase his clarity about what needs to be done and will prevent him from making excuses for not following directions (for instance, "I thought you were asking my brother to clean *his* room").

6. Joy, Joy, and More Joy

One of the most important gifts of ADHD is high energy and emotional intensity. These two aspects can help him pursue what inspires him with a verve other people may not possess. But to enable him to bring these gifts to the fore, you may need to help your child identify what he is passionate about and teach him to respect that passion. You can honor his passions and teach him to use his intense interests as a guide throughout life with this activity, which amplifies and combines your child's interests in creative ways.

The first thing you need to do is observe and pay attention to what your child loves or is obsessed with. Find an activity that combines his diverse interests in a creative way. As one example, my daughter loves Elmo, dogs, drawing, climbing on the couch, and Uncle Eye's CD, especially the song "Flamingo Tango." I created an activity where she was sitting in her Elmo chair (which I put on the couch) surrounded by her favorite stuffed doggies, while she draws and listens to her favorite song.

By encouraging your child to heighten his joy, you are teaching him to live a life guided by pleasure rather than by trying to avoid his fears or run away from punishment. By giving your child deep experiences of amplified joy, you provide a guidepost for him to use as he navigates through his life. You will be teaching him to identify what he loves, what gives him joy, and to follow those feelings of joy. Habits like these will enable him to pursue what he loves, a strategy many people believe is the way to true success in life. In addition, being absorbed in his passions will build skills and the capacity to pay attention and organize himself.

7. Superpower Activate: You're the Champ

ADHD children often feel defeated and deflated by the unavoidable competitiveness of school life. They see other kids sit still, follow directions easily, and complete school tasks without struggle and wonder why they are different. As a parent you can turn your child's discouragement around by teaching him this superpower: the power of praise. This means that when someone else achieves something and your child is tempted to feel envious and defeated, he takes the opposite strategy instead. Teach your child to turn those negative feelings around by saying to himself and/or the child in question, "You're the champ! Great job!" Let your child know that this is a superpower because many people would be inclined to feel jealous and try to tear down others who do better than them. It requires a superhuman power to turn this around by admiring those who achieve things we also want to achieve.

You can also teach your child that he can increase his own powers by asking those who are successful for tips on how they achieved what they did. Tell your child that sometimes you can learn a lot by approaching the person who has what you want and asking them, "How do you do that so well?" This tactic will teach your child to admire and actually learn from those who may be a few steps ahead. Seeking wisdom from others in this way will help turn around not only your child's actual performance, but it can help his social relationships. Many social problems result because ADHD children can feel as though they somehow aren't as good as others and sometimes resort to tearing down those who seem to have it so easy. You can turn all this around by teaching your child about his secret superpower, achieved in three easy steps:

1. Bless those ahead of you.
2. Admire others and say, "You're the champ."
3. Find out how they do it.

8. Practice Receiving

Because your child does have a difference that requires accommodation, he will need to build skills in asking for help and accepting appropriate guidance and resources. You can coach your child in two skills that will be essential for his success in school: asking for and receiving help. This activity will demonstrate to your child the dramatic difference requesting help and getting it can make. You should do the activity for the sake of fun, but later refer to it as a teaching point.

Set up an obstacle course for your child. It can be through a playground, a backyard, or another setting, and it should require him to accomplish certain tasks. Go ahead and time him in the course, or have him race against another child. As an example, on a playground you can tell him to run to the slide, go down it, then dig a hole in the sand and fill it with water, then run to the swing and fly like Superman on it for three swings, then run to the monkey bars and complete those before returning to the start. Whatever creative course you design, be sure to include an activity that will require some tools, like digging a hole and filling it with water. Set your child off and time him or have him race with some other kids. Most likely he will scramble around trying to dig a hole with his hands and then search around trying to figure out how to get water to the hole. When he finishes (or gives up, saying he can't get water in the hole), tell him you'd like him to do the course again, and ask him, "How will you dig a hole and fill it with water?" Be prepared with a toy shovel and water bucket you've kept hidden. Tell him that this time he can come to you and ask for these tools. Let him complete the obstacle course again, this time asking for help from you and getting the tools. Just let him have fun with this game without moralizing, but point out how much easier it is with the right tools. You can refer back to this at a later time to show him how he can help create a supportive environment by asking for what he needs and receiving help. A side bonus to this exercise is that it will help your child use up some of his overflowing energy!

9. Superpower Activate: Adventure Day

Anxiety and fear can do a lot of damage to your child, including holding him back in school and in his social relationships. You want your child to be able to heed appropriate fear without being crippled by a fear of the unknown. One way you can "inoculate" your child from being limited by fear is to tell him about the fear-busting superpower. In this exercise you will set aside a day to have fun exploring something that your child has anxiety about but which can easily be reframed as an adventure. Point out to your child that superheroes have to bust out of their comfort zone every day. Emphasize that this bravery in the face of fear is how these superheroes achieve so much. To further encourage your child to face his fears, try to pair the fear with something your child loves and is passionate about. For example, if your child loves animals but struggles with anxiety in social relationships because of past rejection, you might encourage him to plan a social event that involves animals on Adventure Day.

In preparation for Adventure Day, observe some of your child's fears or ask directly about things that make him nervous. Spend some time connecting with him, talking about how fun and exciting it can be to do new things and how great it is that he will have the chance to activate his fear-busting superpower. Plan Adventure Day with your child or the whole family and support your child, coaching him through the experience of doing something that is a little bit scary.

10. Driving Activity: The Meaning of Life

This is an activity you can do with no extra time taken out of your busy schedule. This one is quite simple. The goal is to provoke exploration of the deeper meaning of life by using drive time to ask your kids, "What is the meaning of life?" Instead of taking the time to listen to music, plan your hectic schedules, or, God forbid, plug in a DVD, use the time to show your child that it can be fun to explore the deeper, bigger questions. For younger kids, you can make the question more concrete, like "What's the most important thing in the world?" or "What makes you the happiest?"

By letting your child know that you are interested in these questions and his answers, you are helping him gain a bigger perspective, which will become essential for him in making choices and maintaining poise in the increasingly competitive and information-rich world. You can also create a journal where you record your child's adorable answers (which are usually a match for any existential philosopher). Recording and reviewing these will help you gain perspective and remember the difference in your own life between a serious problem and an inconvenience. It will also strengthen the bond you have with your child as you share with each other your most authentic selves and learn who your child really is. So many parents are surprised to learn that their children really do have destinies, interests, and perspectives that are not simply reflections of their parents' way of understanding the world. This kind of shared exploration can a... help your child gain perspective about struggles with school or h... social life.

11. Being Special

There is a story about a convicted felon who said that the best time of his life was his criminal trial because he received so much special attention from the judge, lawyers, and jurors. This demonstrates that even highly negative attention can be very rewarding. Part of being a coach to your child is understanding what may be motivating bad behavior and poor performance. In some cases, negative attention that singles him out may in fact be meeting his basic need for being unique and special. One way to prevent your child from seeking out attention in this way is to plan an activity that highlights how special he is. This means doing something with just your child, an activity that involves a treat and extra positive attention.

Many of us use the removal of treats or privileges as a means to discipline our kids when they misbehave. But sometimes taking away treats, attention, or an activity that instills a sense of uniqueness in your child can set up a vicious cycle. He desperately needs to feel important and special, so he reacts by misbehaving even more, both out of frustration and as a strategy to get special but negative attention.

Your child's special activity should involve only your child. If you have other children, you can emphasize to your child that the activity is just for him and not for his brothers and sisters (of course you'll want to make sure each child gets a special-attention activity). Use your creativity in planning the activity, but remember that it could be as simple as taking him out to dinner—just you and him. Emphasize your child that this activity is just to show him how special he is, nd that he doesn't have to do anything to earn it.

12. Record of Delights

Go ahead, admit it. There are times when your child's antics are entertaining and in some way delightful. It is a truism of discipline these days that it is essential to catch your child doing something right. This activity takes that advice a step further, asking you as the parent to observe your child in a spontaneous activity that you find delightful. Watch your child quietly, without letting him know that you're paying special attention to him. Bring to bear all your literary skills and write down your observations and your reactions. Pretend to be writing a literary masterpiece. Later in the day, read out loud to the whole family what you have written. Not only will this intensely gratify your child's sense of self-esteem, but he will realize that you are observing him even when he's not aware of it. Your recitation will show him that his actions evoke a deep response from you. This sense of being observed may motivate him to act in more socially appropriate ways. When he understands the potential his behavior has to impact you deeply he may be more likely to mind his p's and q's.

13. Driving Activity: Brainstorming

Many people agree that the fastest path to a happy and successful life is to find a career where your greatest passions meet with serving the world. Next time you are driving in the car, ask your child to think of an activity that is the most fun thing he can think of and is also helpful to other people. This will give him practice in thinking about both sides of the equation: fun and service. You will need to coach him along—if he says "playing video games," egg him on to think of how he can play video games in a way that would be helpful to others. If he says something like "feed the poor," help him to figure out how he could accomplish this while maximizing his fun. When you come up with an activity, keep taking it to the next level: "How could we, within reason, make this *more* fun?" or "How could we help even more people?" Don't throw any ideas out and keep going to the next level. This process will also teach him the power of brainstorming—everyone contributing to building an idea or plan. Your child will also learn that he can make the effort to constantly improve on his ideas. When you come up with an activity that is reasonable, make a commitment to following through and actually doing the activity. It might be as simple as going to the beach and picking up trash for part of the time or as complex as starting a business that creates fun dance nights for kids in the neighborhood while collecting a fee to participate and donating half of the funds earned to local charities.

14. Interview with a Grandparent

For this activity, you and your child are both invited to interview one of your child's grandparents. Ask the chosen grandparent(s) (or a person of an older generation, friend or family) the following questions: 1) What do you think ADHD is? 2) What do you know about the grandchild's diagnosis? 3) What do you think of the child's behavior? 4) Was there ADHD when you were growing up? 5) How were kids like that treated? 6) What do you think we should do about the frustrations that come with the child's difference?

You and your child should each do separate interviews, preferably with different grandparents or elders. After the interviews, discuss with the family what you learned or what you heard. This activity will forge close connections in the family and most likely will give you a very different perspective on your day-to-day frustrations. I have observed that many grandparents have a special fondness for an ADHD child. They appreciate and see more clearly the gifts of ADHD without being faced with its struggles on a daily basis. Grandparents also have a long-range perspective and can tell you many stories about success and failure across the life span that are not directly tied to academic performance in grade school. I have talked with grandparents who have said that in the past, everyone understood that some of the offending behaviors were completely normal for young boys and girls. Kids who were more hyper than others generally were given fairly benign labels like "ants in the pants" or "class clown." You can share your stories with others by sending them to me at lara@visionarysoul.com and, with your permission, I can post them on my blog to inspire others.

15. The Secret Reservoir

Everyone has untapped resources that they do not know about or are just not using. Some video games require you to have a tool at one level that you had to pick up at an earlier level. When your child is struggling with a problem, you can turn it into an activity—searching for some resource, relationship, skill, or gift he has that can act as a secret tool to help him solve this problem. Tell your child that there is always a secret reservoir that will be useful in solving problems that come along. Talk with your child and help him find what resources he has that he is unaware of. Ask your child, "How do you find your secret reservoir?" Let him generate as many answers as possible. If he gets stuck, ask him the following questions to figure out where to find the secret reservoir:

1. Is there a person who can help you solve this problem?
2. Is there a network of people who could help you?
3. Is there a skill you have that could solve this problem?
4. Is there a gift or talent you have that could solve it?
5. Is there a technology that can help you solve the problem?
6. Is there a resource (Internet, professional) that can help you solve it?

This game can be made fun by making it like a mystery to solve. It will also help your child to gain a sense of hopefulness in the face of his struggles. It will imprint the message that if he keeps looking, he can find a solution to his problems rather than just getting depressed or giving up.

16. The Rock

Whether your child is a fan of World Wrestling Entertainment champion The Rock or not, he can benefit from identifying with and even calling himself "The Rock." At any age, playing pretend games is fun and important for developing imagination. Tell your child to write a story about, or act out, or draw a picture of a superhero called The Rock. You can play along with your child or model for him what

…ualities this character might have. The Rock would probably be immovable, strong, unswayed by disappointment, peer pressure, or whatever else might come his way. The Rock would know that his core gift was strength and persistence and that every challenge was meant to build his strength. The Rock, like any rock, endures all matters of inclement weather and doesn't wear and tear over eons and eons. By enduring this span of time The Rock has incredible perspective on the problems, inconveniences, and temporary setbacks of everyday life. If your child is tempted to say, "Why is this happening to me?" tell him that by confronting and overcoming bigger and bigger challenges, The Rock builds his own powers and strengths, making him the most imposing superhero there is. In this way, your child will see challenges as opportunities for becoming stronger and for showing what power he has.

17. Spidey Sense

In the movie and comics of Spiderman, the superhero has a "spidey sense" that allows him to know when trouble is on the way and figure out how to protect himself. You can play with your child and tell him to practice using his spidey sense. You can sing an adaptation from the refrain from the old TV show, "Spidey Man, Spidey Man, he sees things nobody else can," and repeat with each different sense, "he knows things nobody else can" and smells, tastes, hears, and feels. Ask your child what he can see that no one else can. What can he hear that no one else can? What can he do that no one else can? What does he know that no one else does? Help him begin to trust his intuitions. It can be even more fun to hone his spidey sense by giving feedback. Practice guiding him to sense things that you can check out later to see if he's been right. Review the times when his spidey sense is right and times when it is wrong. Discuss the differences and figure out how he can tell when he is on or off in his spidey sense.

18. Retro Day

The most effective coaches have strong connections to their players. As a parent, your best chance of getting good behavior from your child is for him to feel strongly connected to you. Not only is your child more likely to follow directions if he feels a connection, but bad behavior is often an expression of feeling alone or unsupported. Sometimes our high-tech world makes it almost impossible to really be present with those you love. Whether it's the anxiety to check e-mail or constant access to text messages and cell phones, both parents and kids are challenged to be really present for each other.

A great activity that can help counteract this modern sense of distraction is to plan a retro day. On this day you celebrate a past time, like the fifties, sixties, or seventies, and as part of this celebration, you limit or ban more modern technology. You will discover that operating without your newfangled toys can slow down the pace of the day. But you will also find the slowed pace offers many opportunities for connection. Instead of using the microwave to heat up a packaged meal, take the time to get your kids involved in making a more elaborate meal. Cutting, chopping, stirring, and washing can be a great time to be together and talk casually. You can make it even more fun by giving your kids a sense of history, wearing period-inspired outfits, playing music from that era, and telling your kids about a family-centered way of life. Unplug from your virtual connections and get tuned in to the rhythms of a slower world.

19. Self-Serve Attention

Everyone, and especially kids, has a powerful need to receive attention. You can coach your child to meet some of these needs by giving himself more attention. This can be a great way to help your child feel attended to, and it can also improve his skills at concentrating. After all, he has more incentive to actively pay attention when his focus is himself.

Following is a list of activities that will meet this basic need and are simple to do. Do each activity yourself and then show your child how to do it, giving him some time to practice any or all of these:

1. Give yourself a hand massage. Spend time focusing on your hands and releasing tension through gentle kneading.
2. Just sit still and observe your breathing. No techniques to follow, just notice breathing with curiosity. Try breathing in through the nose and then the mouth. Try shallow breathing and then deep breathing. Just pay attention, and marvel at how you're breathing all the time without having to control it at every moment.
3. Write in a journal. Ask yourself questions. Write down your ideas, thoughts, and observations. Ask yourself what you need and write how you can get those needs met.

20. Siesta

As your child's coach, you will want to teach him to honor taking time out. Whether he spends some time daydreaming or just plain ol' resting, encourage him to take some time off. Time-outs like these have not been valued in American culture, to our own detriment some might argue. But you can introduce the notion of the siesta to your family and gain the benefit of some downtime.

Plan a siesta this weekend, a period when the whole family simply rests. You can tell your child that taking a siesta means he either has to nap or quietly read. This way, he will either be building his reading skills or at least learning the wisdom of honoring the body's need to take a break. The American ideal of constant activity in the service of productivity will take a toll on your child. By creating a siesta, your child will learn to honor his body's natural rhythms and may be encouraged to let his imagination run wild.

Cultivation of the imagination is not only fun, but it can bring great achievement and success. One of the best-selling fantasy books in recent times is a series called *Eragon* (Paolini 2004) that was written by a sixteen-year-old boy. He lived in a small town without much to do, and he said he spent his childhood imagining other worlds and adventures. He created a best-selling book that has become a movie. If you want your child to create new things and be an innovator, it is essential that he learns to appreciate and honor his own imagination and not dismiss it as a waste of time. The weekend siesta can be a time the whole family can use to rest, rejuvenate, and imagine.

Cultivate Your Child's Emotional Intelligence

The greatest gift you can give a child with ADHD—or any child for that matter—is the support they need to become an emotional genius. An ADHD child needs it more than a "normal" child, because she needs help rebounding from the disappointments that come with being different from others. An ADHD child needs to gain *emotional intelligence* (Shapiro 1997)—the ability to know what she is feeling and to use the feeling as information for guiding behavior—because in some ways she is already living in the sea of intense emotions, and learning to swim is an essential skill just for navigating her sensitivity.

WHY EMOTIONAL INTELLIGENCE MATTERS

In addition to offering a greater sense of direction, emotional intelligence will transform bad behavior and many ADHD symptoms into strengths for your child. She will learn how to identify and validate her anger rather than act it out in bad behavior or self-handicapping (giving up so as not to face failure). When your child can recognize and label the full range of emotions coursing through her heart and mind, she will be able to focus her attention when appropriate rather than being driven by her emotions. Intense emotions can be like jet fuel—propelling your child to a constant state of hyperactivity. As your child learns to manage her emotional life, severe symptoms will be translated into emotional cues she can use for guidance.

The activities in this chapter will help your child build her talent in handling her emotions. Every step she takes in building these skills will serve her in every setting for the rest of her life. The quality of her relationships and the success she achieves in the real world will in part be determined by these fundamental skills.

WHAT IS EMOTIONAL INTELLIGENCE?

While many parents focus almost obsessively on their child's intellectual development, research indicates that approximately 4 to 10 percent of your child's career success (Pink 2005) will be determined by IQ (Intelligence Quotient, a standard measure that assigns a number relative to a normal curve describing intelligence).

That leaves the question open—what does determine my child's career success? A big chunk of the answer is emotional intelligence. Emotional intelligence can be developed by validating your child's emotions, reflecting back to your child what she is feeling, and letting her know that her feelings are okay. You can still remain firm that certain behaviors are not acceptable while validating the emotions underneath.

Some of the basic skills of emotional intelligence include feeling mad without lashing out or blaming others and learning to be assertive rather than passive or aggressive. Emotional intelligence means reaching for help when you feel sad and talking through worries with others rather than obsessing alone. Those who lack emotional intelligence may not even know what they are feeling but just feel driven by unknown forces. Some people who lack emotional intelligence know what they feel but express their feelings destructively—either wounding others with words or with actual physical aggression. A major risk of being unable to feel or express emotions skillfully is seeking strategies to numb out feelings, things such as drugs or alcohol or dangerous activities involving spending, gambling, or thrill seeking.

Another significant factor in your child's life success is interpersonal success—how well she gets along with others. My observation has been that a great deal of social success is driven by emotional intelligence. This means that your child's ability to understand her own emotions, read other people's emotions, and express herself skillfully will in large part drive how successful she is in being liked and supported by others. In order to succeed socially, your child needs more than just social-skills training. She needs to master what lies underneath social interaction—emotional exchange.

DEVELOPING EMOTIONAL INTELLIGENCE

In addition to the activities below, which will help guide you and your child in handling emotions more skillfully, the most powerful way to give your child the gift of emotional intelligence is to get it yourself. If you find yourself struggling with issues of emotional intelligence, you would serve both you and your child by working to develop this strength. Many of the activities below will help with that, but you would also benefit by seeking therapy or a support group. The personal work you do can trickle down to later generations, providing healing for those who come after you. Many crippling symptoms can be traced to unexpressed emotions. For instance, chronic health problems have been linked to the inability to express emotions. The ability to feel and express positive emotions is widely regarded as the fulfillment of the purpose of life. The emotional development and personal growth of you and your child is no small thing. It is the essential thing.

EMOTIONS AND BEHAVIOR: MAKING CHANGE FOR THE LONG TERM

In addition to the direct benefits for your child, activities focused on building emotional intelligence in your child will transform your parenting routine. You may have noticed that the behavioral management consisting of things like time-outs and handing out stars for every positive behavior not only gets tiresome but can be short-lived, especially when your child finds herself in a new environment. Whereas giving rewards for good behavior and taking away reinforcers of bad behavior is essential to any program of behavior change, it will not have the life-changing long-term effects that improved emotional skills can offer.

The fundamental reason for this difference is that the lack of emotional skills drives behavior problems. In short, this deficit is the root cause of many offending behaviors. Children are aggressive when they are mad or anxious. Children refuse to follow directions when they are distracted by unnamed feelings pulling them here and there. Children are spaced out when their full attention is on coping with intense emotions they don't understand. If you get to the root of the problem, the behavior will resolve itself.

Think of emotional intelligence as a long-term investment in your child's well-being. Rewards and punishments have a short-term payoff. By working to help your child identify and express her emotions and feel that they are okay to have, you will see benefits begin to accrue over time. It may take weeks or months of teaching your child to say "I'm mad" or "I'm jealous" before the words replace the problematic behavior (something like hitting a sibling). But once she has gained the skill, it will transfer to any setting and will stick with your child for the rest of her life.

In contrast, most reinforcement systems address specific behaviors in certain settings and are often decreasingly effective over time and in different places. These problems are especially exacerbated when dealing with punishment.

PROBLEMS WITH PUNISHMENT

Punishment ("No dessert for you!") may not have the lasting impact on your child's social-skills deficits that you'd hoped for. It may stop specific behaviors in specific settings, but because it doesn't teach right behaviors, positive reinforcement is more important for meaningful and lasting social-skills improvement.

There are some negative side effects of punishment. Your child may begin to avoid situations where she finds herself punished. So, rather than gain emotional or social skills that she needs, she just stays away from people or places where she gets in trouble. This can lead to school avoidance or anxiety disorders when she can't avoid punishing situations. Again, the idea here is that if you don't get to the root of problem behavior (emotional causes), then your child remains bewildered, doesn't understand her own behavior, and feels desperately out of control.

Other concerns with punishment are that your child may simply develop behaviors that help her avoid punishment, such as lying or hiding. Another risk is that your child begins to adapt to punishment, and you have to keep escalating your threats. This kind of escalation can be very destructive to your connection with your child.

In summary, the path to long-lasting change is to guide your child to become an emotional genius. The activities below will help you, your child, and your family gain these fundamental skills and can transform your lives for the better.

ACTIVITIES

The activities below have the power to change the life of everyone in your family. If you were to do one each week, you might find dramatic changes in your own life too. If you weren't raised in an emotionally expressive family, many of these may make you feel very awkward and uncomfortable at first. I urge you to dive in and try them anyway. The more difficult these activities are for you, the more you have to gain.

1. Fun Monitor

The foundation of emotional intelligence is a background buzz of happiness. Even research on learning has shown that endorphins—

chemicals released when we are having fun—promote brain development. In the interest of creating a strong foundation for emotional intelligence, each week you can assign one person in your family to be the Fun Monitor. This person takes on the following role:

1. Plans a fun activity (a family walk, a sporting event, and so on)
2. Tries to think of ways to make regular activities more fun
3. Encourages or provides entertainment through telling jokes, asking others to tell funny stories, or putting on music for the family to enjoy

This new family role, which should rotate every week, will help your family stay on track and can provide a soft landing when kids are struggling with conflicts and demands.

2. Emotional Drumming Game

This is a fun game for the whole family. First, you'll need some drums. You can use toy drums, or you can make some with open boxes covered with taut paper. In a pinch, pots and pans are excellent stand-ins for real drums.

When you've collected a drum for each person, it's time to start drumming, with the whole family playing along. When things get going, you or someone else can sing to the drumming beat, "mad, mad, very, very mad; sad, sad, very, very sad; glad, glad, very, very glad," then point to someone in the family who is experiencing one of these and sing or say, "Rob is mad, mad, very, very, mad. Rob wanted the car and Dad said no; mad, mad, very, very mad." Alternately, a person can call out his own emotion—either of these would work. When a family member is calling out their own emotion, they can express a feeling and what it's about while the rest of the family drums. This helps the person deeply accept and express emotions and creates a culture where these painful emotions are allowed. The drumming can also help your child find a physical expression for feelings, which can be important for younger children. Young kids often don't have sufficient verbal skills to express their feelings in words, and your child may lack the precise nuances for describing what she feels.

You can also use this strategy more organically by bringing out the drum in the middle of a temper tantrum. In this situation, it would be the parent, not the child, who would drum and name the feeling. This act can help your child contain the emotion and you can continue the chant "mad, mad, very, very mad" to give her skills in identifying her emotions and permission to feel them. This could work in two ways. One, by identifying the feeling and validating it in a deeply expressive manner, you can help your child feel okay about feeling it. Two, being so unconventional just might distract your child from her temper tantrum.

3. Slow-Motion Hour

The frenetic pace of life, the constant rushing around, makes it hard for any parent or child to become attuned to her emotions. The flurry of activity, the constant admonishments to hurry, act to actually repress feelings and may even be motivated by the desire to numb our emotional lives. You can raise your child's awareness of how hyperactivity dampens emotions by experimenting with a slow-motion hour.

Tell your child that you and/or the family are going to play a silly game where everyone moves in slow motion. You could choose to eat a meal or play a game during that hour. You can clown it up and make funny slow-motion gestures and draw out your words "sloooowleeeee" to make it entertaining for everyone.

Afterward, ask your child what she felt, thought, or experienced during the slow-motion hour. Many people who try this find that many previously unrecognized feelings come to the surface. Even just breathing more slowly can have the effect of releasing pent-up emotions. When you are in a rush, you and your family will likely breathe more shallowly, which has the effect of numbing us to our feelings. Slowing down and putting full attention on something that usually only occupies one of your many channels of attention leaves open lots of inner space for feelings to emerge. Talk with your family about the experiment, what you learned, and if you would like to do anything differently in your daily routines as a result.

4. Driving Activity: Remember When?

Next time you're in the car with time to spend with kids, play a game of Remember When? You can start out by saying "Remember when ..." and sharing a memory of something that really stands out for you—it can be the best of times or the worst of times, but choose something that was really emotionally charged. Then ask your child and other family members to continue, by sharing a "Remember when ..." story.

This simple exercise will help your kids develop communication skills and help both your child and you learn about what stands out as good or bad, what other close family members' internal worlds are like. For example, one time I was playing this with my son and he said, "Remember when you picked me up before lunch?" I honestly didn't know if that was a good memory or a bad memory and was very surprised that it stood out as a memory at all. I asked him a series of questions and learned that it was a bad memory for him. He didn't like leaving his friends at school and felt sad that he was missing out on lunch just as his friends were sitting down to eat. He remembered it because it was a break in his routine, which came as a surprise to me. I learned a lot about his inner world, his emotions, and how he sees the world. The Remember When? game will give you and your kids a great opportunity to see the world through each other's eyes. It will also help teach your child about how important emotions are and give her practice in understanding situations that evoke powerful emotions.

5. A Trip Down Memory Lane

As the previous exercise will demonstrate to your child, memories and emotions are powerfully connected. You can show your child the power of creating positive emotions by recalling happy memories as a way for her to self-soothe. Looking back at happy times can have a wonderfully lifting effect. One study even found measurable health benefits in elderly people who spent time with the music of their youth and the magazines they used to love (Langer 1989).

Rather than teach her this as a specific technique, you can re-create a specific happy memory of your own childhood—or other memory—to powerfully etch this lesson into her mind. In this way you provide modeling for searching for a memory and then re-creating it. If your child has any inhibitions, you give her permission by going first.

For this activity, choose a specific memory that makes you feel happy and would be easy to re-create in your environment. You will be feeding your sentimentality and honoring the power of memory, connection, and momentous moments. It will be a reminder for your child that she has the power to create happy memories in her daily life. Put on the music and make the foods that remind you of this memory. Dress up as appropriate and make changes in the environment or go to a place where the memory occurred. Re-create the memory and live in it with your child, sharing with her as much as you can about it. It's a way to connect with your child while showing her how she can create a mood with the environment and memories.

6. Poet's Corner

Give you and your family permission to have a family poetry slam. Ask everyone in your family to pick out a poem that they especially like. If your child is unfamiliar with poetry, you can provide some books that will likely appeal to her. You can find children's poetry books at the library. After dinner one evening, or for Saturday night family entertainment, have each family member read the poem they chose. Ask each family member why that particular poem appeals to them. Get a three-ring binder or other folder and save all the selected poems.

Poems usually evoke and reflect deep emotion, so sharing poetry gives your family a chance to dig below the surface and see the depths within each other. If you want to adapt this activity for the car, you can ask one person to talk about a troubling feeling. Then the whole family can suggest poetry lines or turns of phrase that seem to capture that emotion. The person who offered the emotion can say "Yes, that's it" or "No, not quite; it's more like a ..." In this way, the whole family will get a chance to practice putting words to emotions. The greater your child's skill at doing this, the more likely she will be able to translate bad feelings into words rather than bad behavior.

7. Photo-Album Memories

Your children nurse from your emotional life as much as an infant is nourished by her mother's milk. If you track your child's bad behavior you may notice that days when she is especially disruptive may be days when you yourself are under a great deal of stress, out of whack emotionally, or highly sensitive. Many times, these negative undercurrents rise up on anniversaries of some loss or some other reminder of grief. Both you and your child can find relief from any undercurrent of sadness or anger left over from major losses by sharing your personal grief with your family. This will also teach your child how to effectively handle grief. Many parents think they should hide their grief from their kids. However, even when you think it's well hidden, kids can often sense that it's there and will usually go ahead and act it out. In addition, by bringing your feelings of grief out into the open, you demonstrate to your child that sadness and anger are normal reactions to loss and are best expressed and shared with those you love.

You can impress these important lessons on your child by choosing a time to get out a photo album that has pictures of someone you love who lives far away or has died. It may be a family member or friend. Tell your child stories about this person and openly share your feelings with your child. If you feel the need to cry, it's okay to do so. Your child will not be hurt by seeing her mother or father cry. Tell your child that your sadness is a reflection of how much you love this person and that it's a healthy reaction. You can show your child how to recover from sadness by telling her how much your life is better because of this person and that you honor this person's life by remembering how they enriched your own life. This will teach your child the full cycle of coping with loss: grieving deeply and honoring the contribution that person made to enriching your own life.

8. Beach Bum Vacation

An essential skill for becoming an emotional genius is the ability to rejuvenate and restore oneself, honoring the rhythms of a balanced lifestyle. An excellent way to honor this need to play and unplug is to practice small doses of your ideal vacation. You can spend a weekend afternoon enjoying a family "vacation" in your backyard. What, for you, is the essence of a great, satisfying vacation? Many people would say the joy of absorbing sun rays and the leisurely connection of idle chatter with your family. You can re-create this feel by going out into the backyard with your family on a day when there is some sun. Lay out blankets or towels, get out the sunscreen, and take a beach vacation. You can even go all out, making some healthy fruit faux piña coladas, even adding the little umbrella decorations.

This will teach your child the essentials of how to "fill up her own gas tank," encouraging her not to run on empty. In grade schools across the country, young children are sorely overcommitted and can start to feel exhausted by their constant activity. You can use this strategy to teach your child an essential life skill—that they can find a way to meet any need, if only in a small way. If your family desperately needs a vacation but is short on funds, time, or the energy to plan one, you can find ways to meet this need with a little creativity. This will be a powerful lesson to model for your child.

9. Emotional Bingo

Create a bingo card made up of emotion words. You can find both emotional and social bingo cards (for the following activity) at www.visionarysoul.com/bingocards.html. You can either copy the ones here or download them from the website.

On a weekend day, distribute the cards and ask every family member to cross off the box of any emotion they feel that day. Each person should carry the bingo card with them through the whole day. The first person to get all the boxes crossed off in a vertical, horizontal, or diagonal line can call out "Bingo!" winning the game. You should prepare a prize for the winner, which could be something like a book, video, or CD.

This game will help your child get familiar with all the nuances of positive and negative emotions. It will help her attend to her inner world and put labels on her inner experience. It will also promote connection between family members and provide an opportunity to share experiences and emotions.

emotional
BINGO
sad
mad
scared
happy
silly
excited
surprised
jealous
bored
hopeful
lonely
ashamed
disgusted
tired
confident
shy
disappointed
strong
calm
confused
depressed
fearful
defeated
graceful
insecure

10. Social-Skills Bingo

Your child with ADHD may have a very difficult time listening to others and may often interact with them by blurting out what's on her mind without paying attention to what's going on in others. This game will help your child gain the emotional skill of being intensely curious about other people, an ability that can help transform social awkwardness and impulsiveness. For this activity, use the social-skills bingo card below, or download it from the website www.visionarysoul.com/bingocards.html.

Give your child this card and tell her to think about asking other kids at school what their favorites are. Each time she asks another child about a favorite on the bingo card, she can tell you about it later at home, and you can cross off the square together. When the child gets a bingo (horizontal, vertical, or diagonal line crossed off), she wins a prize. This will encourage your child to begin thinking about what other people's interests are. The whole family can join in and play if that will make it more fun for your ADHD child.

11. Relaxation Station

Both kids and parents have difficulty paying attention when they are stressed out. The more stress you feel, the more difficult it will be to concentrate. Simply put, your attention is wasted on the frittering away of focus as it is drained by low-level chronic anxiety and overwhelm. The best preventative medicine for reducing stress and preventing emotional blowouts is training in relaxation. You can make this practice a fun game for the whole family by having each family member create their own individualized Relaxation Station.

SOCIAL
BINGO
favorite toy
favorite animal
favorite color
favorite class
favorite sport
favorite book
favorite movie star
favorite band
favorite music
favorite game
favorite vacation spot
favorite cartoon
favorite store
favorite TV show
favorite movie
favorite video game
favorite song
favorite season
favorite sports star
favorite website
favorite teacher
favorite family activity
favorite sports team
favorite holiday
favorite technology

You can think of it like a "progressive" party, where family members go through each room of the house and get to experience a different form of relaxation. You could also explain it to your kids as sort of like a haunted house, except you go through and get calmed down rather than scared. Just as in a haunted house where those who are creating it try to design the scariest surprises, you and your family should knock yourselves out trying to design the most powerful relaxation strategies. Some suggestions of elements that promote powerful relaxation include:

- Focus on breathing or deep breathing.
- Repeat calming statements.
- Listen to calming music or soothing noises (the ocean, a fountain, and so on).
- Offer suggestions to feel warm and relaxed (for example, imagine sitting by a toasty fire).
- Try some stretching exercises.
- Engage in some downright silliness and laugh your head off.

There are no limits to what you can create or what activities you and your family can design to promote healthy stress reduction. These skills will promote physical and mental health across the life span.

12. Half-Hour of Irritation and Half-Hour of Power

One of the biggest lessons your child needs to succeed in the real world is to press on and finish activities, even when she feels bored or irritated by them. You can teach her this lesson by pairing it with a more fun version and a powerful coaching tool—the Half-Hour of Power. This is a half hour that is fun and sets the stage for success. During the Half-Hour of Power, your child gets the opportunity to indulge in some fun physical or artistic activity. It could be going for a walk, shooting hoops, drawing, or Rollerblading. This half hour is nag free, meaning she gets to do her activity without being told to get back to work or do something more productive.

The other part of the deal is that you tell her she gets this in return for successfully completing her Half-Hour of Irritation. You can work with your child to design what this will be. It should consist of tasks that are not intensely frustrating, not strongly resisted, but that are mildly irritating and require persistent and consistent follow-through. As your child learns to push through irritation, she will gain the skills for persisting in the face of even larger upsets and frustrations. A good choice of activity for the Half-Hour of Irritation could be creating a plan for organizing her week, filing papers, cleaning her room, doing laundry, or if she is mastering some discipline such as a musical instrument, it could be some aspect of practicing that is mildly irritating to her. By pairing these two half hours together, your child will have the motivation to complete the Half-Hour of Irritation while gaining the unstructured time she needs to indulge in what fills her with delight.

13. Wildlife Preserve

In coaching your child to the highest levels of emotional intelligence, she will need to learn that even bad emotions contain important energy that can be used to fuel motivation. Too much energy suppressed in the service of maintaining a bland and unemotional façade can create problems. Of course, it's important to socialize your child. But there also needs to be room for your child's wild side. In that wildness is your child's exuberance, creativity, and connection to nature. Let her growl like a lion, dig in the dirt, or jump around like a chimp. Create an atmosphere and activity where she can let loose, growl, howl, stomp, and romp. This will get her in touch with her wild instincts and provides an outlet for emotional expression such as anger and frustration, whether through a growl or a stomp. You can set this up by encouraging her to pretend the backyard is a jungle or a zoo in which she can act like the animals of her choice. Or, if she sees a movie or reads a book about wildly leaping primates, encourage her to act it out. Many times you can catch her in the act of stomping and ask her to exaggerate it and let herself go in an expression of her innate energy.

14. Emotional Charades

In order to create positive emotions in her life, your child will need to have a reference point to know what it feels like to feel good. For example, if you've never had the pleasure of eating chocolate cake, you might not seek it out. This activity will give your child experience in creating positive emotions so she can know better what she's shooting for and appreciate it more when she gets there.

Your family can play a game like charades, where each family member draws a card with an emotion on it. There are two levels to the game. The simpler game, for younger children, is to just act out the emotion and have other family members guess what it is. The more difficult game is for the person who chooses the emotion to try to create the experience of that emotion in the other players.

Unlike charades, each player can speak in trying to create the emotion in other players. For example, if the positive emotion is pride, a player can say to another, "Your effort today at soccer was A-plus" or, "You're the best mom in the world." The players hear the effort to create an emotion and try to guess what emotion is being evoked. This will help your child learn about how emotions feel while also learning her own power to evoke emotions in others. Emotions are not something that we passively experience, like a TV show flashing before our eyes. We are the directors and producers when it comes to creating emotions. Some examples of positive emotional states to create include feeling: surprised, excited, love struck, hopeful, confident, happy, calm, comforted, supported, blessed, silly, powerful, encouraged, delighted, strong, secure, loved, and successful.

15. Silly Shrugs

Your child may expect you, as the parent, to be all-knowing. She may even feel a great deal of pressure herself to always be in-the-know and may try to hide it when she finds herself at a loss. Of course, it's natural to be ignorant of things sometimes, especially for a child. Therefore, you will be doing her a favor to teach her that no one knows everything all the time, and that it's okay to not know.

The next time your child asks you a question that you don't have the answer to, simply shrug your shoulders in a silly and dramatic way while saying in an even sillier tone of voice, "I don't know." Clown around for a while and say it over and over again, making it funnier and funnier. By teaching her that there is no shame in not knowing, you are opening her up to be a better learner and problem solver. In order to solve a problem, you have to recognize that you need more research or more information. If your child is free to acknowledge when she lacks knowledge about something, she will feel better able to go after the information she needs without shame.

When you play this game, go ahead and invite your child to join you in a series of silly shrugs. While this can create a great opportunity for enjoying some silly laughter and help take the pressure off you and your child, the activity itself is also a great stress relief. The simple act of shrugging your shoulders can relieve built-up tension and can be a type of yoga or body therapy that targets and alleviates the overwhelming feeling that the world is on your shoulders. When you add the phrase "I don't know" to the physical relief, you and your child will have a powerful cue to use in difficult situations to gain perspective on the true meaning of education and learning.

16. Read Me Like a Book

This game will help you, your family, and your friends develop one of the most valuable emotional intelligence skills—empathy. Especially for a child with ADHD, who is prone to impulsive and aggressive behavior, empathy can help to ease social relations, as your child will be more apt to sense and care about how her actions affect others.

This fun game can be played with the whole family and with friends. For this activity, have everyone write the titles of their five favorite books on a piece of paper. Have everyone fold up the papers and put them in a hat or bowl. Each person takes a turn, pulling out a piece of paper and reading the five titles. Then, the "chooser" tries to guess who wrote down those titles by considering what kind of person would love those books. You need to think about the interests and personality of each person when trying to determine who chose which books, an effort that helps to promote feelings of empathy.

It can be fun to figure out who selected which books, but this game asks you to go farther. Like Sherlock Holmes, the famous fictional detective, you are to try to figure out what it's like to be the kind of person who would choose those five titles. How do they think and feel? What's important to them? Each player is challenged to come up with more and more details about the person who chose the five favorite books in question. When the player has given a great effort, other players can join in with guesses about who the book-lover is or other ideas about what that person must be like on the inside. The game can finish up with the person who actually chose the five books coming forward and offering insight into how accurate the comments were.

17. Driving Activity: Sedona Method

This exercise is an adaptation of an emotional-release technique called the Sedona method (Dwoskin and Canfield 2003). It can be fun and entertaining for the family to do while driving in the car with some time to pass. This game will build emotional intelligence by giving your child practice in feeling and releasing emotions. It's wonderful to be able to name feelings and to accept them, but releasing them is also a fundamental skill. One person starts with a feeling that is bothering them. Another person in the car asks the following questions about the troublesome feeling:

1. Where in your body do you feel the feeling?
2. Close your eyes and imagine that you can dive into your body and feel that feeling. What does it feel like? Is it light or dark? Does it have a texture, feeling smooth or rough? Is it hot or cold? Does it move fast or slow?
3. Can you imagine that feeling leaving your body and flying out the window?
4. Do you want to keep the feeling or let it fly away?
5. If you want to keep it for now, where can you put it later (when we get out of the car or when we get home or when we arrive at our destination)?

Although this exercise can be used to help release troubling emotions, it can still be helpful even when the person playing declines to let the emotion in question fly away. If the person isn't ready to let it go, they have still made progress in clarifying and naming the feeling. If there are others in the car, each one can ask the person the same set of questions. It can be helpful to go through this process many times.

After one person goes through a round of these questions, have a conversation about how it's helpful or not helpful. Each person can take their turn, having an opportunity to present a troublesome feeling and go through this round of questioning by other family members.

18. Paint a Pretty Picture

This activity is not really about painting. It's about helping your child learn how to create a vision of where she wants to go in life. You and your child can play together to create a collage of photos that expresses who and what your child wants to be. Too many times, the child can only picture being what she is now, and in the case of a child with ADHD, that may reflect poor grades and other rejection experiences. You and your child can get original and create a list of what life would feel like and look like if she achieved what she wanted. You can choose photos of colleges your child might like to attend, or a person in a career your child is interested in, or athletes winning gold medals, and so on. Once you have selected and cut out a lot of inspiring photos representing the life your child can create, paste them on a posterboard and hang this creation in your child's room. This will help to raise her expectations for herself and offer her a clear picture of where she wants to go.

19. Yoga Jam

This activity will prove to your child that she can manage her activity level and stay in control. This exercise will show your child how to channel lots of energy but also will show her that she has the power to change her tune when she needs to. When you do the activity in a fun context, she will learn that she can stop and do something different, slowing herself down or speeding up if she needs to.

Put on some fun music and dance with your kids. Or you can encourage her to dance by herself or with friends. Stop the music and show her a yoga-like pose for kids. This could be as simple as bending over and putting her hands on the ground. By stopping and starting the music, your child will alternate between fast dancing and slow stretching movements. The process of alternating back and forth gives her practice in speeding up and slowing down her tempo and physical movement. This will increase her ability to believe she can control her movement and will hopefully transfer to the classroom, for example, when a teacher asks your child to sit down or slow down. Do many rounds of back and forth and your child will learn:

1. Skills for shaking out the sillies
2. Skills for modulating her energy
3. Confidence in her ability to switch back and forth and control her activity level

20. Driving Activity: Name That Brain Game

Most people concentrate better when they are relaxed. For a child with ADHD and its attendant concentration difficulties, finding ways to relax is especially important. One great way to increase a sense of relaxation is to practice meditation. Meditation is really just a way of bringing your focus to something simple and paying attention to that one simple thing for a period of time. This activity can reduce tension and bring a sense of calm, even to a child who often feels her attention pulled in many directions at once.

You can teach your child the basics of meditation by playing the Name That Brain game. Tell your child that the brain plays a number of games, but the two biggest brain games are thinking and feeling. You can review the difference between thinking and feeling for your child. Try saying something like, "Thinking is when you have ideas or you are talking to yourself on the inside. Feelings are those forces that seem like they push and pull us around, like when we talked about mad, sad, glad, and others." Then, while you're driving in the car, you can ask everyone to go around and name their current brain game. At that particular moment in time, are they thinking more or feeling more? This is a central meditative practice to become aware of mental and emotional processes. It will help your child gain some distance and therefore control over thinking and feeling. A central achievement of meditation is to have a feeling rather than *be* a feeling, or have a thought rather than buy into the thought.

For older kids, you might try adding the following labels: "thinking," "feeling," "planning," and "worrying." You can go around the car a few times and see if people's brain games change. If someone gets stuck, you or other family members can help figure out what label is right or create a new label.

While this activity is a fun way to help your child tell the difference between thinking and feeling, the real point is to give her an introduction to meditation, where she learns to observe her thoughts and feelings.

3

See the World Through Your Child's Eyes

This chapter brings us to another fundamental paradigm shift. It is a shift from demanding your child conform to your worldview and expectations to giving yourself the chance to see the world from your child's eyes. When you take the time to see the world the way your child does, you will be giving a great gift to yourself.

This shift doesn't mean you stop using discipline or quit helping your child build skills to follow directions. It means that you balance your need to enforce your authority with honoring your child's idiosyncratic way of experiencing the world. Part of your child's unique worldview will be informed simply by the fact of his being a child. Another part of his perspective will be informed by predictable differences related to the diagnosis of ADHD. Some of the ways in which your ADHD child is different is his need for stimulation, change, constant activity, a hearty dose of nature, and inventiveness rather than passive learning.

RELEASING PERFORMANCE DEMANDS

Trying to meet constant, unrelenting demands for performance is difficult for any child or adult, but more so for an ADHD child. An excessive focus on academic grades when your child may not be well-suited to the current educational system can wear down his emotional reserves. I believe that it is reasonable for you to hold high standards for your child. But, when you lose perspective and emphasize performance demands over being present with your child and letting him have time and space for play, he will predictably chafe at the restrictions.

Part of seeing the world from your child's eyes means honoring his need for play. If you give your child both time for play and the gift of your presence, you will be filling up his tank, so to speak, for his continued effort toward achievement. It's not reasonable to have 90 percent of your interactions with your child involve nagging him to follow directions, do his schoolwork, and clean up after himself. In order to listen to you, your child has to feel connected to you. In order to feel connected to you, your child needs to be fueled up by moments, minutes, hours, or days of being present with you without any demands being made on him. Like different levels of octane at the gas pump, you can give your ability to be present with your child a much-needed boost by making the leap toward understanding why he does what he does, why he wants what he wants, and why he needs what he needs.

FROM PETTY COMPETITION TO OUTSTANDING EXPRESSION

It's too easy for parents to get caught up in petty competitions. These can be about whose kid is the smartest, whose kid does best on the soccer field, or whose kid is the most popular. We all want our kids to be happy, healthy, and to live up to high standards.

Pay attention to how much time you spend comparing your child to other kids his age. Excellence does not have to be defined in comparison to others. Also notice if you are expecting your child to excel at too many activities. If so, he may be wasting vital energy that could be used for deep absorption in one area in which he's both interested and gifted.

It may be that the capacity for outstanding expression, the sort of giftedness that makes all of us wonder, is depleted by running around from one brain-building competition to another. Perhaps by frittering away your time and energy by following the crowd in the competition du jour, you miss your child's unique form of expression. It might be that you are running from tutoring program to football game at the moment your child is inspired to be an artistic genius. Maybe you're determined that your child will match your focus and discipline in playing the clarinet, when he would find great release and expression in something like martial arts, a physical activity that could help him settle down to do his homework.

When you begin to see that your child's needs, interests, and talents are highly idiosyncratic but deeply meaningful, you can step back from your fears about him falling behind and step up to discovering his arena of outstanding expression. Remember that once he forges the link to his outstanding expression, it will provide fuel for all other arenas of motivation and achievement. The expression of his interests and gifts will energize him, not deplete him.

BROADEN YOUR DEFINITION OF SUCCESS

One of the most important paradigm shifts you can make for your child is to break out of your narrow definitions of success. Some parents work on models that go like this: "If my child doesn't get all A's in school and ace the SATs, he won't get into the best universities and won't go on to be the doctor, lawyer, CEO, or senator I want him to be." This construct may be a slight exaggeration, but it represents an all-too-common deep-seated and toxic anxiety that a child will fall off the earth if he steps off of a narrow path of unrelenting and ever-increasing accomplishment.

If you were to bust out of this narrow and suffocating mold for your child and yourself, what permission would you start giving yourself and your child? Maybe you would let your child quit clarinet lessons and take tae kwon do instead. Maybe you would free up your weekends to pursue your own interests if you stopped pushing him to participate in the marching band even though he's complained about it incessantly. In reality, success in life is so much broader than parents' narrow definitions. You cannot protect your child from the disappointments and frustrations involved in making dreams come true. Your child's greatest dreams may lie in fields outside of your narrow definitions of success. You may worry that your child wants to be an artist or athlete and wonder how he will support himself with interests like these. Give your child permission to love what he loves and do what he loves. Gain a broader perspective and remember that this passion fuels his ability to build skills and will increase his motivation in other arenas. If you allow your fears to cut your child off from his passion ("He won't be able to support himself"), you are also cutting off your connection to him and his connection with his energy source.

ACTIVITIES

The activities in this chapter will help you step outside of the day-to-day struggle to fit your child into a cultural mold that even experts argue is quickly being broken. By trying out these activities, you will be able to take a larger perspective and release yourself and your child from power struggles. Remember that the more you honor your child's perspective, the more connection you forge with him, and the more likely you are to gain compliance. The irony is that when you release your demands for compliance and take a moment to take a deep breath and allow yourself to wonder rather than to stew in despair, you gain "relationship capital." This means that when you drop your end of the tug-of-war rope, the struggle stops. The gratefulness and loyalty you will reap by exploring your child's inner world will pay off in terms of his willingness to listen to you and eagerness to follow you.

1. Organic Play

Research shows that when a child is deeply engaged in examining, exploring, and playing, he is building brain connections. This sounds wonderful, but what about all those times your child is deeply engaged in activities that make you nervous—climbing trees, for example. For this activity you are going to practice checking your anxiety through one of the following strategies. When your child is pursuing an intense area of interest, you will let him proceed without interfering. Your only job in this situation is to control your anxiety. Here are a few strategies to help:

1. **Financial concerns.** Omit one expensive present, toy, or class, and each time your child engages in an activity that you feel is wasting money (cooking something that won't be edible, ruining clothes by painting or hiking, and so on), mentally chalk it up to the thing or activity you didn't buy.

2. **Concerns about messes.** If you're tempted to interfere with some of your child's activities because they make huge messes, try to remember the brain-building benefits he's gaining. When you remind yourself of what he is learning, it may be easier to resign yourself to cleaning up and/or supervising your child as you help him clean up after himself. Many times parents create just as much work for themselves by stopping activities that the child is absorbed in, only to then have to create some new project to entertain the child.

3. **Safety concerns.** Many of your fears are likely based on the realization that the things your child enjoys

doing do pose some risk if they are unsupervised. The antidote here is to simply pay attention. When you might ordinarily tell your child to stop climbing the tree because it's dangerous, try allowing him to climb with your close supervision and guidance. If he gets into trouble, you will be there, ready to help, and he will gain all the benefits this activity has to offer.

2. If They're Happy and You Know It, Take a Break

This exercise is similar to the first one, but you don't even have to check your anxiety. In this activity, if your child is busy and happy, you get to take a break and meet your own needs. Sometimes parents are worried that the activities their kids naturally choose aren't suitably brain building or competitive, so they feel the need to constantly create structured activities. When you cut out the need for performance demands, you will make your life easier. If your kids are happy and occupied, take a moment to rest or otherwise meet your own needs. Don't feel that you need to intervene. You can sing to the tune of "If you're happy and you know it, clap your hands," but substitute "If they're happy and you know it, take a break."

Sometimes parents who work away from home are anxious to make all the time they get to spend with their child "quality time" and are limited in defining quality time as requiring their active involvement. If you want to be involved, remember that "attention is the most basic form of love; through it we bless and are blessed" (Tarrant 1998, 6). Don't feel you need to be busy or directly involved with your child. Just by quietly observing him you can nurture him and meet his needs, as well as your own.

3. Abundance Mentality

ADHD kids struggle with performance demands and the belief at school that there's just not enough to go around. Some kids get the good grades, and some just don't. One way you can help your child to heal from this mentality is to give him experiences that help him to trust that there is abundance in the universe. There really is enough to go around—there is no shortage of the essential goods. The activity below is designed for younger children but can be adapted for older kids by encouraging them to create their own water park in the backyard.

In this activity there is no competition. Your child gets to play for the sake of enjoying the water, exploring his creativity, and the license to get wet and messy. Kids inherently enjoy making a mess, and this will give yours the chance to do so without worry.

This is an activity that has no performance demands, no rules to follow, and no better or worse. It's the water fun activity. What you will need is:

- A bucket of water
- A turkey baster or any other water-squirting utensil
- A package of two hundred paper cups

Fill a bucket with water and give your child and any accompanying friends other tools that can be used for scooping, pouring, or containing. Show them how the turkey baster works and how fun it can be to squirt into the cups. Give them five cups. If there is more than one child, they will probably start stealing each other's cups and fighting over them. But since you have two hundred cups, you can keep giving them as many cups as they want. Give them more than they ask for. Show them that the world is generous and not stingy. This exercise allows for creativity since there are no rules. They can play without any performance demands or worries about spilling water or making a mess.

4. Nature Soak

Research shows that kids with ADHD who get out in nature improve in their ability to concentrate and follow directions (Taylor, Kuo, and Sullivan 2001). But many of the activities kids typically engage in out in nature include performance demands or competition. Create an activity out in nature that has no rules, plans, or competition. A simple activity is a nature soak where you simply spend time in nature soaking up the natural beauty. You can lie on the ground and watch the clouds go by, or simply walk in a park with no goal or purpose.

You can also create a nature adventure by going out in the middle of the rain, wearing rain gear and letting you and your child jump in puddles and feel the rain on your face. You might also find a safe place to walk at night and take the time to gaze at the stars. By seeking out experiences in nature you may usually avoid (for instance, you might ordinarily avoid being in the rain), you will help meet your child's need for seeking stimulation, which may be the root of a lot of the behavior that gets your child in trouble. If you honor that your child needs both nature and these walks on the wild side, you can feed that need through excursions into alternative weather conditions or unstructured activities that you habitually avoid.

5. Guru Day

In this playful activity, you can get dramatic and give your child the chance to pretend he is a guru. Give your child a guru platform and a guru outfit. Ask him some of the tough questions you are struggling with. You will get amazing answers. Even if you don't, you will be entertained, and your child will gain a sense of his capacities and a belief that you value what he thinks. This exercise will demonstrate the power of expectations: if you convey to your child that you expect that he will have useful answers to real-life concerns, he will, in many cases, live up to those expectations.

You can also adapt this exercise for the car. You can talk about your real-life problems, puzzles, and pressing concerns and ask him what he thinks. Kids with ADHD are typically better at these types of challenges than at the more-traditional methods of testing knowledge in an academic environment. ADHD children tend to be interested in and very good at solving real-life problems. By showing your child you are interested in what he thinks you can also add to his sense of self-esteem. If he offers any suggestions that you do use and find helpful, be sure to make a point of sharing with your child the impact of his help.

6. Punk Quartet

For this exercise, you will create an activity that takes a seeming expression of defiance and combine it with one of your own interests. This will allow a creative outlet for one of your child's activities that you typically look down upon (but not one that is outright self-destructive). This experience will go a long way toward keeping you connected to your child even though his behavior troubles you at times.

For example, if your child likes punk music and you play classical cello, you can combine these interests by having a jam session with your child where you play the cello and he gets to improvise punk lyrics or go all-out on the drums. Or, if you are a hard-nosed businessperson and your child just wants to draw cartoons all day, help him create a business plan for earning money from his cartoons. You might ask him to draw a cartoon to market your own business. If your child daydreams all day and you're a sports fanatic, take him to a sporting event, but rather than focusing his attention on the game, let him space out and ask him on occasion what he is experiencing. You will most likely find that he is paying attention to parts of the event you never even noticed or thought about. In this way you share the activity you enjoy while allowing him to have the experience he wants. And you might very well learn something from him. If your child likes to play video games too much and you're worried he'll never be able to make a living, ask him to do some Internet research on the people who get paid to create video games, the people who run companies that make video games, or the people who get paid to market them. You can ask for him to come up with a list of ten people who make money in the video game industry and e-mail or call at least one person on the list. Some universities actually have majors in gaming, and you could ask your child to find and research those programs. These examples can be adapted to whatever interest of your child is a thorn in your side. Find a way to integrate your passions and your child's.

7. Information Seeker

In this activity, you will interview your child as if for a magazine article. Many parents feel that they know all there is to know about their child. But if you take the time to ask deep and probing questions, you may be surprised at what you learn. You can choose as your topic something your child loves to do, does well, or something he does differently than anyone else. Ask him why he does it this way, why he loves the object of his passion so much, and what his secrets are for being so good at what he does. In this way, rather than automatically assuming you know what your child does and why he does it, you are opening yourself up to learning about how the world looks from your child's eyes.

You can also apply this activity in more spontaneous situations. If you find yourself angry at your child for something he's done, maybe something that looks like defiance, remind yourself to seek more information before you express your anger. Before getting angry and handing out punishments, ask as many questions as you can think of about why your child took these actions, what he was trying to do, and what was going on in his mind. You may find information that completely eliminates your anger. You may even find that you are able to translate your understanding of the behavior from defiance to self-reliance. For example, you may find that what looked like direct defiance of your request that he clean his room was really a result of his curiosity at finding a broken toy he wanted to fix. Instead of getting to the cleanup, he sat right down to work with the toy, using his creativity to see what could be done to repair it.

It's also possible that you will still have cause for anger and a need for discipline. However, the step of asking questions and gathering information before expressing anger will still have allowed you to connect more with your child, which will increase the effectiveness of your discipline.

8. Back to the Future

This activity is an elaboration of the one you just read about. In this activity, rather than seeking to learn about what's going on in your child now, you will seek to set in motion the forces of positive expectation. This activity will help shift your focus, and that of your child, from petty competitions to the outstanding expressions of his deepest gifts. To begin with, you will ask your child what dream he would most like to come true in the next five years. Five years from now, where would he like to be and what would he like to be doing? Make sure you encourage him to dream bigger and bigger. Then settle on a concrete goal that would be a great passion and great accomplishment for your child.

Next, you can pretend you are an interviewer for your child's or your own favorite magazine. Pretend you are interviewing your child five years from now after he has accomplished this dream. Ask him a series of questions like:

- How long did it take you to make this dream come true?
- How did you accomplish such a great feat at your age?
- What advice do you have for others who want to do this?
- What was the hardest part of making your dreams come true?

- What did you do when things got tough?
- How did you keep going when you felt disappointed?

You can also make up your own questions. You could even write an actual article based on your interview and give it to your child to read. It will serve as a great reminder when he gets discouraged or needs motivation.

9. Media Star

This activity relates to the themes of this chapter in a number of ways. First, it builds on the Back to the Future exercise in encouraging your child toward outstanding expression rather than petty competition. Second, it expands the narrow definition of success many parents have and introduces your child to a possible career choice in media. Because ADHD kids have so many interests but get bored when they stay with one topic for too long, they would be great working in the media, where the job is to cover late-breaking stories that are changing every minute.

This activity involves creating a multimedia presentation of a story your child is interested in. You can elaborate on the results of the preceding exercise and choose to cover your child's accomplishment of his five-year goal. Or, you could choose another event or topic of interest to your child. Then, assist him in creating a representation of this breaking story using writing, pictures, video, or all three.

You could take the article you wrote in the Back to the Future exercise and work with your child to turn it into a full magazine feature, taking photos and working with formatting and other creative products. He could do the formatting and arrangement of visuals using the family computer or by cutting out the article and pasting it on construction paper and pasting photos with the text. He could also take photos and create a collage. If you have other equipment such as a video camera, your child could create a TV feature of this news piece. You could explore how to create a blog and use that to get the word out. You could use a tape recorder and create a radio interview of the news feature. The more forms of media your child learns to use to express himself, the more positive expectations you are helping him create. And the passion he has for the story he is telling will fire his enthusiasm to learn the technical aspects of reporting.

10. Spa Hour

One of the main themes of the paradigm shift toward seeing the world through your child's eyes is changing from parenting in the service of performance demands toward parenting in the service of your child's needs. This includes giving yourself permission to let your child be pulled by his pleasure. In this activity you and your child create an environment that promotes healing and self-care. You can include products such as candles, soothing music, scents, oils, or a foot-care package you can find at any drugstore. Whether your child is a boy or girl, they will benefit from the recreation of a soothing environment where you practice one or more skills of caring for the body. Together, you can soak your feet in warm water with oils or scents while playing music in the candlelight. You can practice applying a facial mask, or if you have a child who is squeamish about that, you can just show him basics of skin care. You can purchase a back scratcher or back roller and practice on each other. Use the time to have fun and connect with your child. Don't try to solve any problems or address difficult issues. The goal is just to have fun with your child and connect.

You can also create a basket for your child with some of the self-healing products you find and enjoy. You can gather them all in a basket and place the basket in a visible location to remind you and your child to practice self-care. You can include short meditation books, a pack of cards with yoga poses (I've seen these at stores like Whole Foods), and a prayer card or some sacred object that you find healing. You might even keep the spa basket near the TV and encourage your child to indulge in self-care rather than playing video games or watching TV. Through this home-spa experience you can help translate your ideas of what relaxation means from passive consumption to active self-healing.

11. Dream Circle

In many traditions, communities come together and share their dreams with each other. If you start a game of sharing dreams with your child and family, you can gain a clearer vision of the inner world of your child. Although sometimes dreams seem meaningless or silly, when you begin to share dreams, you give yourself the opportunity to learn valuable insights about each other that you might not have found otherwise.

Sometimes dreams can have the deep impact of revealing to parents the very unique character of their own child. Oftentimes, children have interests, needs, and destinies that are far from their own parents'. Sharing dreams can provide a window into these differences. Realizing your child differs from you may be hard at first. But try to honor these differences in the service of meeting his needs and allowing him to succeed.

You can start a tradition of sharing dreams on weekends. It may start slowly, as some of us have trouble remembering what we dream. But if you are consistent in asking for a dream exchange with your child, it is likely that you will begin to remember more. It's okay to remember and talk about a dream fragment or just one feeling or image that stands out if that's all you or your child can remember at first. You don't have to be Sigmund Freud to make sense or meaning out of dreams. Just let yourself have fun and don't take it too seriously. Things to notice are how seemingly small events can loom large in your child's mind. You may be surprised that an event that seemed minor to you needs to be talked about with your child. You may also notice how your child's world is intensely relational—meaning that they are incredibly sensitive to connection. Your interest in your child's dream world will increase his sense of closeness to you and increase his own awareness of inner forces.

12. Driving Activity: Transcendental Daydreaming

John Muir, the great naturalist, believed that "transcendental daydreaming is fundamental, essential, the substantial enterprise of life" (as quoted in Sinetar 2000). For the ADHD child, seeing daydreaming as an act of self-reliance rather than one of defiance is a huge reversal and will probably be wonderfully liberating for him. Children with ADHD often get into trouble for spacing out in structured environments. When your child is daydreaming, he is usually deeply in his imagination and processing relationships and events rather than tracking what's going on in the environment. This activity will demonstrate your respect for this mode of engagement.

Next time you are in the car with time to spare, discuss the quotation above with your child. Involving other siblings and the other parent would be great. Here are some questions to jump-start the discussion:

- What do you think "transcendental daydreaming" means?
- How could daydreaming be the fundamental enterprise of life?
- How can daydreaming help you succeed?
- Why does the world need people who daydream?
- What great people can you name who are known to have been daydreamers?
- What people do you know in your personal circle who daydream?

By having this discussion you will get your child thinking about how the common daydream can fuel the achievement of his goals. You will encourage your child to begin to honor his natural inclination toward dwelling in his imagination. As you begin to honor and accept this valuable skill, your child will feel more accepted and connected to you, improving your relationship and his behavioral acting out.

13. Driving Activity: What the World Needs Now

One big worry for parents of ADHD children is that their kids won't be able to succeed in the world. If you commit to the idea that your child's differences are just that—a difference and not a disorder—you begin to nurture your child's uniqueness. To take it a step further, many leading-edge thinkers are taking seriously the idea that the dramatic changes in the world and economy will require just such a difference that many ADHD children have. In *A Whole New Mind*, Daniel Pink writes, "[t]hanks to an array of forces—material abundance that is deepening our nonmaterial yearnings, globalization that is shipping white-collar work overseas, and powerful technologies that are eliminating certain kinds of work altogether—we are entering a new age. It is an age animated by a different form of thinking and a new approach to life ... [a]nd the capabilities we once disdained or thought frivolous—the 'right-brain' qualities of inventiveness, empathy, joyfulness, and meaning—increasingly will determine who flourishes and who flounders" (2005, 2-3). These capabilities map almost exactly onto the gifts I outlined in *The Gift of ADHD* of creativity, exuberance, interpersonal intuition, emotional sensitivity, and ecological consciousness.

For this activity, discuss what the world needs now. Using the ideas of *A Whole New Mind* quoted above, talk about how your child's unique gifts meet the needs of the world. Try to work toward reframing your child's "defiance" into self-reliance and successful strategies. You can start with the quality of inventiveness and try to see how your child's difficulty following directions may be related to that quality, for example. The next activity will offer a companion exercise to elaborate on your child's inventiveness.

14. Invention Convention

In this activity you will have a "convention" of sorts of your child's inventions. You can open it up for family and friends. Like a museum curator, put on display all the inventions or acts of creativity your child has produced. Many ADHD children excel in drawing, music, or performance arts like dance. In addition to the collection of creative expression you already have, prepare for the Invention Convention by trying to see how seeming acts of defiance are in the service of inventiveness. In *A Whole New Mind*, Daniel Pink quotes an inventor, Trevor Baylis, as saying, "the key to success is to risk thinking unconventional thoughts. Convention is the enemy of progress. As long as you've got slightly more perception than the average wrapped loaf, you could invent something" (2005, 133). Be inspired by this quote and translate your child's oppositional behavior into this sort of inspiration. Your child's creativity may be in a realm that you consider as just child's play and not worthy of the title of inventiveness. But whether it's making elaborate train-track configurations or tinkering with your mechanical objects, many of your child's activities, especially when they are "misbehaving" in some way, can be seen as creating something new. If your child doesn't do his homework but creates a masterpiece landscape out of Legos, take a photograph to display in your Invention Convention. For one week in preparation, don't rebuke your child for the energies he channels into arenas that aren't necessarily related to school or other disciplines. Honor these efforts by recording them and saving them for display. If your child tells a story, write it down and put it in a frame to show it off. If your child creates a dance performance, write a review and share it with him. Many great inventors get lost in their enthusiasm and find it difficult to pay attention to other demands. Whenever possible, take advantage of the times when your child doesn't follow directions to see if the activity he is absorbed in can be seen as a form of inventiveness.

15. What Should My Child Do with His Life?

Many parents have quite a narrow definition of what career success means for their children. This kind of limited expectation leads to undue pressures on the child to select an area of interest that conforms to conventional notions of prestigious careers. For this activity, you and your child can work together to create a list of careers that sound like a lot of fun to your child. Try to put your expectations and anxieties about your child's future on hold for this exercise and just explore the career possibilities. As an example, if your child loves action and adventure and thinks being a policeman would be a great idea, don't squash that idea by saying something like, "That's too dangerous! Pick something else." At this point, you are simply trying to gather career choices that thrill your child and fit with his intense interests. Also, try not to worry for now about how much financial success a certain interest might have. Just let your child research areas of interest—artistic expression, sports, trains, cars, military—whatever your child thinks would be great.

Once you have picked as many career choices as possible, ask your child to select five that seem better than all the rest. Do more research together on these five, asking your friends and family if they know people who do these jobs and even trying to get an interview with at least one person who works in one of your child's top five picks. Your child should do the interview, but you can help by facilitating the meeting. For example, you might invite the person over for lunch. If your child is younger, you can help by trying to find a way to spend a day around people who do what your child loves. It may be as simple as going to a train museum if your child love trains, or taking him with you to the car repair shop if he loves cars. If your child completes an interesting interview, you can send it to me at lara@visonarysoul.com and I can post it on a blog to share with other readers.

16. Creative Complaining

Instead of nagging your child to stop complaining, experiment with honoring your child's complaint and translating it into constructive creativity. If your child complains about basketball practice, seriously reflect on the possibility of quitting. Why is he going to practice anyway? Why is he playing basketball at all? Whose agenda is the activity fulfilling? If he complains, explore alternative possibilities. Are there activities that you push and your child resists that are really meant to meet your own needs? If he complains, consider this possibility.

If your child complains that he never gets a moment to rest and relax, choose one day to experiment with changing your schedule so there is more downtime. Or choose a week and let him help create a schedule. Choices that initially feel hard, like dropping activities, can surprise you by providing great, unexpected relief.

Find a way of translating one or more of your child's complaints into an action or activity that respects the complaint's content. Experiment with seeing the complaint as an action plan. You don't have to make a commitment to the change on a long-term basis, but explore what it feels like to do things differently. Instead of telling your child to stop whining, give in for a short while and offer him the sense of power that comes with being heard. This compromise may even just reveal that what he wants doesn't work, but at least your child will have the sense of being heard and will learn for himself that what he wants isn't reasonable. It's also possible that your child's complaints will transform your life in positive ways, freeing you from unreasonable expectations that hold both of you back.

17. Mix It Up

As you begin to focus on creative expression over petty competition, you will be heartened to realize that being able to combine diverse domains will be a much-valued skill in our current culture. In December of 2006, *Time* magazine ran a cover article on the school of the future and the need to integrate across disciplines (Wallis and Steptoe). A fun way to begin preparing your child for this demand is to reflect on your family's main interests and brainstorm on how to "mix it up" or spend time in new settings and doing things that are quite different from what you usually do. As an example, if you and your child love the mall, plan a nature trip. If your child is a tree-hugging nature lover, figure out how to have a fun afternoon at the mall. If your child is a sports fanatic, take him to an art exhibit or introduce him to a performance art that combines athleticism and creativity. If your child is a snob, take him to a garage sale. If he's a slob, take him to a beauty salon for a stylish haircut. Many breakthrough books (*The World Is Flat* [Friedman 2006], *A Whole New Mind* [Pink 2005]) have highlighted adaptability as the key trait for success in the future. As your child learns to explore polar-opposite domains, you are preparing him to succeed in a global and increasingly diverse world.

An additional benefit of this activity is that when you and your child spend time out of your familiar places, you experiment with being out of control in a healthy way. When you are in a new setting, you don't know all the rules—you are outside of your regular routine and have given up some measure of control. Some of your ADHD child's out-of-control behavior can be seen as actively seeking out the experience of being out of control. The drive to seek stimulation and break out of rigid patterns causes a lot of the symptoms of ADHD. If you can meet that need for stimulation and loss of control in healthy ways, you can practice a sort of preventative medicine.

18. Landscape Artist

A main theme of this chapter is that what looks like defiance can be seen as self-reliance. When you take the time to examine your child's perspective when he doesn't follow directions, you will often find he is seeking to meet a need that is predictable in the ADHD child. A lot of bad behavior in ADHD kids can be explained by their increased need for physical activity and their desire to be in nature. Kids don't clean their room or do homework because they are itching to get outside and get moving. Once you meet this need, you may have more luck getting him to follow through on your agenda.

You can improve your child's skills at following directions (and his enthusiasm in doing so) by giving him projects to do outside. You can ask him to act as your landscape artist, helping you to design and implement a plan for your yard, garden, or community. This will combine physical activity with being outdoors. You can ask him to plant some flowers or pull weeds. You can give him a project involving designing a garden area using plants, stones, and other materials. If you give your child the opportunity to be outside and use his creativity while keeping busy, you will be meeting many of his needs. You can even give your child a problem to solve, like deciding what to do with an unused or overgrown bit of the backyard. Give your child a chance to come up with answers and propose projects to solve real problems.

19. Music Appreciation Class

One of the benefits of trying to see the world through your child's eyes is that you will forge a strong connection with him. But this connection must be earned. It may require you to take a very different attitude than you normally hold. You could find it helpful to think of yourself as an anthropologist, observing your child quietly, with deep curiosity but no judgment, trying to make sense of the world in which his behavior serves an important function. When you begin to develop this skill, whole new worlds will open up for you. I remember one time my son was unrolling paper towels across the whole house. I paused a moment before rebuking him, calming myself down and asking him what he was doing. He told me he was building a train track for his imaginary train. I decided to demonstrate respect for his imagination and let him "waste" the paper towels.

In this exercise, you will seek to learn about something your child is obsessed with that you actively dislike. You will ask your child to teach you about something that you typically nag him about—it might be his fashion choices, the music he listens to, a video game, or even a TV show. Act like an anthropologist and try to understand why the behavior that is irritating to you is so meaningful to your child. If the offending behavior of choice is listening to music that you find execrable, ask for a music appreciation lesson.

20. Bring Your Child to Work

If you break out of narrow competition and begin to believe that you are helping your child toward outstanding expression, many new doors of opportunity will open up for you. As a parent, you will realize that you want to introduce your child to as much of the real world as possible so he will have a chance to excel and solve real problems. With this paradigm shift, you may realize the wisdom in having your child actually do some of your professional work. This is different from doing chores—I'm not talking about passing some dreary task off to your kid. Instead, find a real task involved in your professional life that is appropriate for your child to do. It could be licking envelopes that need to be mailed or helping you build something or even a research task, if your child is old enough. Older children have basic skills in Google and Internet research. Your child will love feeling like a part of your work life, and you will love showing him the tools of the trade. Many parents feel distracted in the time they spend with their child because they're so often thinking about work. You can have your child help you with your concerns and chalk that up as quality time for both you and your child.

4

Stand Up For Your Child's Strengths

In this chapter you will learn about the power of becoming a fierce advocate for your child. This means that in interacting with friends, family, schools, and health care professionals you need to take an active role in translating your child's behavior as strengths. The activities in this chapter will help you overcome the urge to apologize for your child and cringe in shame at her behavioral problems.

A recent study demonstrates how fundamental it can be for your child's well-being for you to become a strong advocate. The study showed that children with ADHD diagnoses and typical behaviors often become stigmatized, with those around them preferring to keep their distance (Martin et al. 2007). This study shows how a lack of intervention can result in a vicious cycle developing. Your child's behavior can lead to stigma, which leads to social isolation, which leads to increased symptoms.

DON'T APOLOGIZE—ADVOCATE

The most important thing you can do is to be on your kid's side. This means that you make it your goal to help your child come out looking good. This doesn't mean that you don't practice good manners and teach your child to apologize if she has hurt someone, but rather that as a general strategy, you need to actively reframe your child's behaviors. Any chance you get, you should try to explain behavior in as positive a way as possible. Below, you will learn precisely how to do this, including looking for external and temporary explanations for bad behavior and seeking internal and global explanations for good behavior.

As frustrated as you may get with your child, remember that staying very closely connected to her is the most effective way to minimize acting out. In the heat of the moment, the first intervention should be to get down to your child's level and look her intensely in the eyes with care, concern, and love. Touch her in a calming and loving way. If you can remember this as a first approach to handling any behavior such as whining, wanting something she can't have, or acting out, you will minimize many problems.

In addition to reframing bad behavior and maintaining your close connection to your child, you can actively search for a gift that your child is expressing and help others see this gift. Rather than cringing at her hyperactivity, try saying, "Isn't she the spunky one!"

When her emotions are bursting forth, help others see how intense and sensitive she is. If you cringe, you are likely to evoke a similar reaction in others. If you see and mention the gifts, others will too.

CONNECT TO YOUR CHILD'S TEACHER

Your child's teacher has a great deal of power in your child's academic achievement and general level of happiness. You will want to work closely with the teacher to tweak classroom consequences and help him or her see your child's gifts. Invite your child's teacher to begin asking, "What's right with this child?" and turn around a possible negative cycle. One simple change that I advocate for and explain more fully in *The Gift of ADHD* (2005) is for parents to ask teachers not to take away recess from an ADHD child who doesn't follow directions. The reason for this is that the symptoms of ADHD improve with physical activity and time spent in nature. Taking away recess is like taking away the child's medicine.

There are many other ways to assist your child's teacher by using your knowledge to suggest the most effective strategies for helping your child. As a parent, you often know what works and what doesn't work with your child. By having the courage to trust yourself and speak out, you can greatly benefit both your child and her teacher.

In the next section you will learn how to adopt an *optimistic explanatory style*—meaning that you explain your child's behavior in the most positive way possible—to help others understand your child. Once you master this style, you will want to encourage your child's teacher to adopt the same way of understanding your child.

THE OPTIMISTIC EXPLANATORY STYLE

Research over many decades has shown that applying an optimistic explanatory style can help depression and health problems and even extend the length of life (Giltay et al. 2006). Being positive means explaining bad behavior in a different way than you explain good behavior, and the guidelines below can help you adopt this strategy. Basically, the idea is to give your child as much credit as possible for good behavior and to try to find causes outside of your child for bad behavior. Then, in chapter 5, you will learn how to balance the need to be positive with the need for your child to accept responsibility.

How to Explain Bad Behavior

A positive approach means that you point to the context of a behavior rather than blaming your child when her behavior is bad. Four places to look for what is causing your child's behavior include:

- Seek the external, not internal
- See the situational, not global
- Understand that it's temporary, not permanent
- Reframe behavior as reflecting a positive underlying trait

As an example, if your child disrupts class, you might determine that other children were talking and your child couldn't resist leaning over to listen to what they were saying. You can also point to other occasions when your child has made contributions to the classroom environment. You would want to look at any stressors that may be in play that could provoke the behavior. For instance, maybe the disruption occurred during her birthday week, making her more excitable than usual. You might also indicate that the child's disruption of the class was driven by her intense interest and curiosity about the interpersonal interactions of others, pointing out that this quality is a great gift to be cultivated.

One way to find external, situational, and temporary causes of behavior is to ask your child. If you ask her to explain her behavior, she will often point to environmental triggers. Even if she cannot yet point them out specifically, by listening to her closely you can usually determine what some of these may be. Your first reaction should be to ask for an explanation and to listen rather than to start blaming her or defending her.

How to Explain Good Behavior

The flip side of the positive thinking style is to make sure you explain good behavior as being typical of who your child really is. Some guidelines to help you do this are listed below. Please note that while the content of these guidelines is the same as those above, what you are looking for in good behavior has reversed from what you are looking for in bad behavior. For example, rather than limiting explanations to a particular situation, you will want to explain good behavior as typical across many domains to yourself and others.

- Seek the internal, not external, causes of behavior
- See the global, not the situational
- Understand that it's permanent, not temporary
- Find the positive, praise the positive

As you start getting in the habit of looking for good behavior, it will become easier and easier to do. Each time your child completes a project, you can make sure to notice it and tell her that she is a focused and highly motivated person. By explaining her successes as being essentially who she is, she will begin to believe it and will act in ways consistent with these core beliefs. You can also improve behavior and advocate for your child by offering her and her teacher examples of other situations in which she showed similar behaviors. You are in effect saying that this positive behavior transcends this one situation, whether it is in school, working on a creative project, or participating in a team commitment.

In addition to pointing out as many settings as possible where you have observed this positive behavior, you can comment on how often you have noticed similar behavior. In short, you want to present a positive representation of your child's behavior for yourself, your child, and your child's teachers, friends, and family, reminding them and yourself that she behaves well many times and in many places.

ACTIVITIES

The activities in this chapter are meant to both entertain and enlighten. They will give you strategies for becoming an advocate for your child and train your child to advocate for herself. Some of the activities will help you see your child for what she is—a delicate child who is, by definition, immature. Some of the activities will illuminate just how unreasonable the demands placed on your child may be, positioning you to advocate for realistic standards in multiple domains. The activities will give you the broader perspective you will need when navigating complex interpersonal and institutional landscapes.

1. Toot That Horn, Ring That Bell

For your child, the process of reflecting on her own behavior, realizing that this behavior was noteworthy, and telling someone else about the achievement can be a far reach. Your ADHD child is driven by whims and pushed on by an inner motor that leaves little time for pausing to reflect and seek attention for completed projects or other accomplishments. ADHD kids are so excited that when they do something worthy of remark, they tend to forget about it and just move on to fulfilling the next creative whim or impulse.

However, the ability to pause and let a teacher or parent know about successes will be essential to succeeding in the world. In short, your ADHD child, while gifted in so many ways, usually is not interested in or skilled at playing the "credit game." The credit game is the one that most people play too well, sometimes living their whole lives seeking credit from others and forgetting to check in with their own internal compass to see what would be the most personally fulfilling course of action.

The defiance of an ADHD child is often a reflection of a fierce self-reliance. A consequence of this quality is a disregard for seeking praise or credit for herself. You can train your child to gain this skill by starting at home with an exaggerated reward system. You can set up a "toot-your-own-horn station" with a kazoo, a recorder, a drum, a bell, and a dry-erase board. Give your child examples of what sorts of accomplishments count: finishing a project, following directions, creating a piece of art, practicing a skill, reading a book, or having a great idea. Tell your child that when she does any of these she can go to the toot-your-own-horn center and write the accomplishment on the dry-erase board, celebrating by creating a loud display of musical exclamation with the instruments you've gathered. You may need to start by asking her at regular intervals if she did anything to toot her horn about and run through a list of activities that would count.

2. Points on the Board

Research has shown that for marriages to stay healthy, positive interactions must outweigh negative reactions five to one. In couples where this ratio is consistently out of balance, there is an increased likelihood of divorce (Gottman et al. 2002). It seems reasonable to think that for a child who has ADHD, this would be a good number for parents to shoot for, too. This means that while you identify weaknesses and resources for addressing those, you should balance that out on a scale of five to one with compliments and expressions of tenderness.

You can make a game out of this with your child by telling her about this magic number and the need to get "points on the board" by finding five ways to support her. For each positive gesture or comment you make, you get one point. Sometimes an ADHD child can fall into two traps: feeling totally beaten by life because of her struggles, and/or covering over real failures that need to be addressed. By letting your child know that for every problem that needs correction there must also be points on the board, earned by acknowledging positives and giving support, you can defuse both of these traps. If you can turn this into a fun game and the idea really hits home with your child, she won't need to hide her failures because she will know that there is a built-in system to help her rebound. You can keep a dry-erase board on the wall to use as a scoreboard, and each time you have to address a problem you can write it on the board under a minus sign or the word "Challenge." Then make a big fuss about how it's your turn to find five balancing statements or actions to get points on the board. You can count these under a plus sign, the words "Already Fabulous," or whatever works for you. Make the game fun, for example by kissing your child five times and saying, "Okay, we're back in the game!" Or you can find five positive things that weren't canceled out by the problem behavior and share those with your child. Use your creativity to find ways to get points on the board. While this activity is ostensibly about the parent earning points, you can also let your child know that in her own self-talk, she should try to maintain a similar ratio. The game can gradually evolve toward targeting the child's self-talk and keeping a separate scoreboard on hand for her to keep track of her personal points.

3. Fixing the Blame Game

In life, teachers, kids, or other parents may blame you or your child for situations related to ADHD behaviors. You can immunize your child and yourself to this kind of blame by teaching your child to "fix the problem, not the blame." By practicing this game with your child, you will remind yourself how unhelpful blame can be.

In this activity, you and your child will practice challenging blame. Kids of all ages love to play pretend games. Use a favorite pretend character or a beloved pet and play a game of Fixing the Blame. Create a story line that is funny, entertaining, and appropriate to your child's age. For example, if you are playing with the dog, you can point at him and say, "It's Rocco's fault! All the cookies are gone because Rocco ate them all." Then guide your child to create silly stories about why, even if Rocco ate the cookies, it's not his fault. You can try a story like superhero Rocco valiantly eating all the cookies to save everyone else from getting fat. Or you could say that Rocco ate all the cookies because he saw ants in the cookie jar and he didn't want anybody eating ants. The stories can be as silly as you and your child like and don't have to make real-world sense.

When confronted with a real-world situation where your child is blamed, you will want to keep in mind that appropriate manners come first, such as a direct apology if appropriate. You will also want to apply some of the ideas learned about coaching your child if the problem results from behavior that is repetitive. However, if (as in many situations) no one was hurt and your child is being blamed for being disruptive, the skills she will learn in this silly storytelling game—finding good intentions and recognizing that the complexity of any situation almost always transcends blaming one person—will serve her in real life by helping her find deeper intentions and environmental provocations.

4. That's an Interesting Perspective

A few years ago, my husband and I went on a guided tour through Jerusalem. The tour was led by a Jewish woman, and the people on the tour came from many diverse faith backgrounds. I remember overhearing the tour leader's response to a man telling her that since she wasn't Christian, she would suffer dire consequences. I reflected deeply and with great admiration on her reply to this insensitive comment: she said, "That's an interesting perspective." I realized that her many years of guiding ardent believers from different faiths had given her an incredibly broad perspective on other people's beliefs. You, too, will need this high level of diplomacy when dealing with your child's health care providers, teachers, and other family and friends.

When you advocate for your child, remember the uncommonly wise words of R. Buckminster Fuller: "You never change the existing reality by fighting it. Instead, create a new model that makes the old one obsolete." You will want to embrace this approach by creating an intense visual picture of your child's gifts for teachers, health care providers, and others close to your child. When they offer harsh criticism, you can say, "That's an interesting perspective, and ..." Then proceed to paint a compelling new picture of your child that will replace or augment the old one.

5. Shrinking Violet

Sometimes what gets lost in the apologies and advocacies for your child is how precious and delicate your child is. In all the bluster of trouble and in the face of your child's high energy and impulsiveness, parents, teachers, and care providers forget that the child is just that—a child. A child is clumsy and immature, by definition. At some point your defense of your child has to be not that she is perfect, but that she is, after all, only a child. Or maybe she is just reflecting the American can-do attitude, where we're all supposed to be bold and fearless pioneers. Whatever bravado your child may adopt, always keep in mind the delicate fragility that you might remember from when she was a newborn.

For this activity, think of a term of affection that you used when your child was a newborn or some other term that evokes the intense sensitivity of your child's inner world and level of development. Schedule an hour or make it a regular occasion where you cater to your child's highly sensitive nature. Call your child the nickname that evokes her complete dependence on you and others for care, and do what it takes to let her know you will protect her from the harsh realities of the world for this short time. Let her be a shrinking violet; don't push her into the world or egg her on to solve her problems or become a better person. Convey to her that you are her fierce protector and offer comfort in a way that is familiar to her. It might be sharing a cup of cocoa and talking about her feelings or cuddling up and watching a favorite movie. Create a gesture that can become a tradition or regular activity that shows how much you realize she sometimes needs to retreat from the demands of the world.

6. Mama-Bear Roar

While you want to honor your child's tenderness and at times cater to it, you also want to help her build skills of self-protection. A mama bear is an animal that is emblematic of the instinct to fiercely protect one's young. Think of stories you have heard or seen on TV of a mama bear acting decisively if she feels her young are threatened. Not only do you want to adopt this passionate kind of response, but you want to teach your child to find this feeling within herself so she can defend herself when attacked. This activity is not meant to teach you or your child physical or emotional aggression, but rather to help her connect with the instinctual mama bear in each of us.

If you have any personal anecdotes to share with your child about a time when you became fiercely protective, she would love to hear it. As an example, I remember when my son was first born, and I was overcome with how powerful this force can be. I was in a parking lot with my son in a stroller and someone raced past me too closely for comfort and pulled into a parking space. I followed her and forcefully reminded her to drive more slowly and carefully. This behavior was totally new for me, but it represented a primitive force for protecting my young. Share a similar story with your own child as a template for how she needs to speak up to create a positive and safe reality for herself at school, on her sports team, and other places.

For this activity, you can have fun with your child practicing a Mama-Bear Roar. This will connect both you and your child to this protective energy. You can role-play a difficult situation in your life or your child's where you or she feels threatened. One of you can play the role of the person who is threatening, and the one who is threatened can practice a deep roar that a wild bear might make. Have fun, letting yourself get loose and getting in touch with your power and animal instincts. You can switch roles so each of you gets to practice the Mama-Bear Roar.

7. People Watching

One aspect of adopting an optimistic explanatory style is to find environmental explanations for bad behavior. As a simple example, if your child doesn't follow directions, it's pessimistic to say, "It's because he's a bad kid" (internal) and optimistic to say, "It's because he is stressed out" or "It's because Mommy and Daddy had a fight" (external). You can practice building the skill of seeing the external causes for behavior by playing a game with your family where you observe others and try to find a reason in the environment for what they are doing. You can do this when you're talking about others, reading a story, or even watching TV.

For example, you can go to a mall with your child for some people watching. Together you can try to explain why people are doing weird things. If you see a teenager who is dressed outrageously and acting obnoxiously, ask your child why she thinks he's acting that way. She may say something about the teen himself, for instance that he's crazy or mean. Guide her to practice coming up with an explanation that puts the cause in his environment. You might come up with an example, like maybe his parents don't give him any attention and he is simply trying to get more attention from his parents or others. You can apply this to bad behaviors you see on TV or when talking about neighbors, friends, or family. Don't forget that you use external explanation for bad behavior only. For any good behaviors, you try to find internal explanations (for example, you got a good grade because you're smart). In chapter 5 you will learn about the importance of flexible thinking and find an activity that allows you to consider the possibility of examining contexts at the same time you teach your child the importance of taking personal responsibility.

8. See for Yourself

If you have any doubts about the power of optimistic thinking, try an experiment to see its impact for yourself. Think of the most positive words you can about someone you deeply respect. Write them down. Now write a letter addressed to yourself, pointing out your great qualities and using the very same words you used for your respected friend. Sign the letter with something like "Your Biggest Fan." You can send the letter in the mail to yourself or put it in a place where you'll find it a week later and read it then. Notice your reaction when you see those words written to you. When you read those words, let your imagination soar. What do you think you are capable of? If this ability to motivate and inspire is so easy to activate, I wonder what in the world we are doing letting our kids and ourselves be crippled by harsh judgments.

Now try adapting this activity to your ADHD child. Can you write her a letter or send an e-mail with a wide-open affirmation of all that she is capable of? When she receives it, ask her how she felt when she read the letter or e-mail.

9. Role Reversal

One way for you to become a powerful advocate for your child is to try to separate out what emotional issues are yours and which are your child's. For example, you may be disappointed in your child because you wanted her to do or be something that you were not able to do or become. Or you may want her to reach some height that you did achieve, but which is not consistent with your child's profile of strengths and weaknesses. It is not a failing unique to parents of ADHD kids but a universal phenomenon that we get our selves mixed up with our kids'. This activity will give you some insight and guidance for separating your self from your child.

Next time you have a recurrent struggle or fight with your child, break the pattern by switching roles. If you sheepishly realize one day that you are acting in the way you chide your child for, use that opportunity to jump-start this activity. For example, if you are driving your child to school one day and you begin to crave that double, extra-hot, hold-the-whipped-cream latte even though you know it's no good for you, you can both express yourself and play your child's role in begging for something she knows is off-limits. Try to imitate your child's tone, words, and mannerism, wailing, "I want my latte! I want it now! Pleeeaaase?!" Make it clear that you are doing a silly imitation of your child and invite her to play the parent role. She will probably delight in throwing your own words of restraint back at you, and you will have fun acting out the desperate pleas and actions she uses when she doesn't get what she wants. This game can be a humorous way to see the universal struggles of parenting and discipline from the child's *and* the parent's perspective. It will also reveal how, sometimes, what you think you want for your child can be all mixed up with what you actually want for yourself.

10. Taste of Your Own Medicine

This is the only activity in the book that doesn't involve your child directly, but it will greatly impact your relationship with your child nonetheless. For one full day, write down all of the guidance you give your child on that day. This could include reminders about eating healthy, finishing projects, specific answers to questions, common struggles ("Hurry!"), and your expectations for your child ("We don't act that way"). Record as accurately as possible your words, your attitudes, and your expectations for your child. If you offer words of instruction multiple times, keep a running tally of the count.

Write yourself a letter with the same guidance you offer to your child, but offer it to yourself in a context relevant to your life, including your current struggles and successes. Read the letter and determine what parts of the guidance you offered your child would be important for you at this point in your life. Take those messages to heart.

You may also want to note guidance that, on reflection, is unreasonable for you or your child. You may realize when you look at the tally that you asked your child to hurry twenty times that day. When you are on the receiving end of this advice, you may decide to make some changes.

This activity will help you accomplish two things. First, it will help you to examine the ways you may have a lot of intensity around issues your child has that are also your own. Secondly, it will help you advocate for your child because you will be able to more clearly determine the reasonableness of the demands and expectations that you, your family, and your child's teachers make on your child.

11. Creative Writing Activity

Take out a piece of writing paper or a journal. You will be writing a creative response to the following story:

> *You overhear the conversation of two elderly women (or men, if you are a man). One woman says, "Youth is wasted on the young! If only I'd known then what I know now." The other woman says, "But we can't go back." You interrupt, curious and slightly desperate to know what wisdom they could share. You implore, "But you can tell me, and I'll do it differently." One of the two women looks at you and says, "You have to learn by making the mistakes yourself, and being human means you will have to make the same mistakes more than once." The other woman looks at you and says, "It's all about priorities." Then the women go on to offer you more advice …*

Now write in your journal or on the piece of paper what the women tell you about your life problems right now and your concerns about your child.

The next time your child asks you to tell her a story, tell her this story of the two elderly women and include your creative completion. If the child is older, you can tell her the story starter and let her finish the story.

Many times the struggles with your child and other people involve achievement expectations—for yourself and for your child. Often the efforts to access resources for your child can devolve into power struggles. When you feel lost in these battles, you will serve your child best if you can remind others and yourself of the highest priorities. It may be as simple as letting a child's academic performance take a backseat to forging a strong connection with your child and preserving her self-esteem. Once you are clear about priorities, some conflicts and struggles may fade in intensity.

12. Under Pressure

For this activity, get out a journal or a pad of paper, a pen, and a kitchen timer. Sit down with your child and set the timer for fifteen minutes. Write a list of all the expectations you have for your child, then have her write the expectations she has for herself. These should be expectations in the realms of scholastics, personal care (sleeping, hygiene, health), physical fitness (sports, exercise), recreation (playing and fun), family, and any others that seem relevant. When the kitchen timer goes off, compare notes. Discuss the differing expectations you have and where the expectations are similar. Without crossing any expectations off the list (except duplicates), put them all on one piece of paper. Copy the final list so each of you has your own list. Then set the timer for another ten minutes. This time, each of you will (on separate pages of paper and at the same time) go through the list and put the amount of time each day your child would have to spend to fully live up to the expectation (for example, six hours a day at school, three hours a day for homework, and so on). When you're done, each of you adds up the number of hours in a day your child would need in order to live up to the expectations you have for her and she has for herself. You will likely find that the number is far more time than is available each day.

This activity isn't meant to improve time management, and it isn't intended to solve the problem of how to fit everything in one day. The exercise demonstrates that when you pile your expectations on top of your child's, you likely end up with unreasonable demands. This will give you some compassion for your child's sense of being overwhelmed and will help you connect more closely with her.

13. Breathing Room

In this activity, you will use the combined list of expectations from the preceding exercise. You and your child will practice downgrading expectations to preferences. For one week, pick one expectation on the list each day and play with telling your child it's a preference rather than an expectation. Ask your child to notice how her life is different when this changes. For example, on Monday you might say that being an excellent soccer player is no longer an expectation you or she should hold for herself—it's simply a preference. Does that change her feelings, her life, her schedule? Maybe the switch results in you two deciding to skip soccer practice and make a family dinner rather than getting fast food, like you normally would. Each day of the week, pick a different expectation to downgrade to a preference and notice the changes it makes in your life and her life. You don't have to make any permanent changes, but by playing with expectations, you will see how they put pressures on your life that you have the power to change.

14. The Tried and True

Sometimes it can be hard to advocate for your child when you are downright frustrated with her. You may have so many stressors in your own life that having to go to bat for your child yet again begins to feel like a burden more than an honor. This activity will remind you what it's all about and reconnect you with your deepest, most profound sense of connection with your child.

Maybe you already do this every day. Maybe you haven't done this since your child was a newborn. But for this activity, you will set an alarm or make a point of staying up late to watch your child sleep. Plan to watch her for at least ten minutes. There is no agenda—just watch your child sleeping. When you are done, write down the new perspective you have. Write down any thoughts or feelings that emerged.

The next day, tell your child you checked in on her while she slept, just watching her for a few minutes. Share with her your thoughts and feelings. This will strengthen the connection that you will need to bring momentum to your efforts to advocate for your child. This tender experience will also refresh your perspective and remind you of your child's innocence and her need for a strong protector and defender.

15. Creative Appreciation

One of the foundation stones of becoming an advocate for your child is to connect with her teacher. Research demonstrates the importance of the teacher's perceptions of your child in your child's success (Rosenthal 1987). You can demonstrate your appreciation for your child's teacher by working together with your child on a creative project to give to her teacher.

You can take out a blank piece of paper and write a heading like:

- "For my favorite teacher"
- "You're the best"
- "Thanks for your support"

You and your child can work together on an art project, creating a collage or a drawing that expresses the positive qualities you see in your child's teacher. This will be a chance for you and your child to discuss all of the teacher's positive qualities and work together on a creative project. This will help you both stay positive and increase your chances of working with your child to connect with her teacher to find the best opportunities to get your child's needs met. Even if you have had many frustrations, it is important to stay focused on the positive.

16. Driving Activity: Gossiping

This is another activity that you can easily do while driving in the car. In fact, you're probably already doing this, but you can use this structured activity to learn what gossip really means and how you can use it to help your child.

Ask your child to talk about her friends or family members, inviting any comments she has about them. Listen carefully to your child's observations and comments. Keep in mind that whatever your child is gossiping about is usually some quality that she is struggling with herself or a quality she needs to learn to develop in a healthy way. What catches our attention in others is either a projection (we see ourselves in others) or it shows what we resist in ourselves. For example, if she talks about a friend being too pushy, it can mean either that she, too, struggles with being pushy, or more likely that your child needs to learn how to be more pushy and give herself permission to express this quality in a healthy way. Since you know your child well, it will probably be easy for you to determine which the case is. But you can also ask questions like, "How would you handle that situation?" to get a feel for what skill your child needs to gain. Once you know what she is lacking, tell her a story of how she could express that quality in a positive way and give her permission. For example, you can encourage her to "throw her weight around" if you sense she needs to be more proactive in social and other situations. You can ask teachers to help her develop this quality if they see an opportunity arise.

17. The Secret Garden

This activity involves a family movie night. Find and rent the movie *The Secret Garden* (1993) and watch it with the whole family. Have a discussion about the movie following your viewing. One point you might discuss is that the main characters are three ten-year-old children. I was impressed with the productivity, imagination, and healing power of these children who had no formal structure to their day. I'm not holding this out as an ideal but as a movie that can help manage your anxiety.

Many parents feel that they have to structure each moment of their child's life, paying for formal lessons and schlepping the child to each brain-building activity. *The Secret Garden* beautifully illustrates the power of children to use their imagination and to create activities that fuel their development without pressure to perform.

Ask your kids what they think of the movie and listen carefully to their responses. The movie provides a stark contrast to the fast-paced, high-technology life of today. The kids in the movie don't have TVs, cell phones, iPods, video games, or any of the modern conveniences. Two of the movie characters are given complete freedom to structure their days. The movie illustrates the power of nature and friendship. Does the movie trigger longing for this sort of freedom or a negative reaction to life without modern conveniences and technology? Because the movie beautifully depicts childhood in another time and place, it offers a new perspective from which you and your child can reflect on your current life and realize the choices involved in your lifestyle. If your child is at least nine years old you can read the classic book the movie is based on, *The Secret Garden* by Frances Hodgson Burnett (2002).

18. "Curiouser and Curiouser"

The gold standard in Western education today is performance. In times gone by, the cultivation of curiosity was the gold standard of true education. The smart person was not the know-it-all, but rather the person with boundless curiosity who was pulled by a desire to explore and to know. Think about the difference between being pulled by curiosity and being pushed by the pressure to perform. When advocating for your child, you can emphasize this difference and stake a claim to cultivating curiosity. A cover article in *Time* magazine called "How to Bring Our Schools Out of the 20th Century" argued that in order for the educational system to keep up with the rapid changes of the digital age, schools, teachers, and parents will need to begin to help students acquire the skills to cultivate curiosity (Wallis and Steptoe 2006). There is so much to know, now that we are becoming a global civilization interconnected by technology. To get a handle on all this information we increasingly need to be able to think outside of the box. The abilities identified in the article, such as finding new sources of intelligence and using emotional intelligence, can all be fueled by curiosity.

You can help your child by sharing her areas of intense curiosity with her teachers. Sit down with your child for an hour and ask her what she really wants to learn about. Create a collection of areas, topics, subjects, and questions that are of intense interest to your child. Let her spirit soar with delight at learning about the world rather than letting it be crushed by the demands to compete. You may even want to take a trip to the library and find the *Time* article cited above, sharing it with teachers and your child. You and your child can discuss the article and what it means for her future.

19. Driving Activity: Translating Trials into Training

While you are driving in the car, talk with your child about a current and pressing challenge she is facing. Maybe she's struggling with poor performance in school or feeling rejected by a peer group. Tell your child that every difficulty in life helps us build skills, and those skills can serve us later in life. Try to figure out what skills your child has to build to cope with her current difficulty. As an example, if your child doesn't quite fit in with the cool kids, she might be learning to develop self-esteem based on uniqueness rather than conformity. If your child is struggling in school, she might be building the skills of persistence and hard work. Or she might be learning that she can't compare herself to others. If your child needs to ask for help, you can tell her that learning to get the help you need is one of life's most valuable skills. Find a way to translate her struggles into a form of training. Then try asking her what sort of career choice or lifestyle requires the skills she's learning from this challenge. If she is in training, what's she training for? For example, a person who learns to work hard, who knows how to ask for help, and who can keep her nose to the grindstone without looking around to compare herself to others might be a good leader, manager, or executive. Take some time to wonder about the possibilities together.

20. A New Attitude

So many times we only offer praise to our kids or to others for achieving some sort of specific success, such as getting an A in school. In this activity you will offer your child a series of compliments based on an appreciation of her struggles. Below are some examples:

- I see how you're keeping your chin up in the face of your struggles at school.
- I admire how you just keep trying, even when you're disappointed.
- I know it isn't easy for you in gym class, but I think it's great that you keep practicing.
- Even though these are hard times, just talking about them together will bring us closer. I like how you're willing to share with me.
- I'm proud of you for trying something new.
- If you just take one step at a time, this will pass over time. I admire your persistence in getting through it.

- This is really an epic struggle, but if you keep going you will gain strength. Your fighting spirit is really impressive.

If you can learn to appreciate your child in her struggles and in her triumphs, she will learn to have compassion for herself and others. Many of life's struggles don't have easy answers, but moving forward and facing them head-on will often result in triumph over time. When your child is struggling with intense feelings of disappointment or failure, help her out by recognizing what she is doing well in the situation. Through this sort of modeling she can learn to become her own gentle coach.

Exercise Flexible Thinking

The focus in this chapter is to help you juggle the competing demands any parent feels. You want to hold high standards, but you can see how the competition and pressure these standards can produce take their toll on your child. You know it's best to stay positive, but you want your child to deal with life's realities and be able to tolerate frustration. You're committed to advocating for your child, but you worry that being his champion means he won't take responsibility. This chapter will help you balance all of these competing demands and others.

I'm now going to begin challenging you to start asking a new question. Instead of either high standards or connecting to your child, you will begin to ask, "How can I have both?" Each time you are confronted with one of these dilemmas, push yourself to look for a solution that honors both sides of the tension. In doing so, you will learn the art and science of flexible thinking. Flexible thinking means you realize that in some cases you don't have to put your chips down on one value over another. Flexible thinking means that you have the ability to find a way to honor seemingly competing demands.

How can you connect deeply with your child and yet still set strict limits? Some of the activities below will guide you toward answers to this question. One of the answers is that the more deeply connected to your child you become, the more you see his side, the more leverage you have to enforce standards and limits. Another piece of the puzzle is that your child will push limits just to get the much-needed attention he is seeking. If you give him what he really wants—someone trying to see from his perspective—he won't need to push limits to get your attention.

You may be afraid that seeing your child's side will compel you to always do what he wants. You have the power to work hard to see your child's perspective while choosing limits and standards that are different from your child's. But as a parent, you always win by making a great effort to see the world from your child's viewpoint, whether or not the actions you take cater to that perspective.

WHO'S THE BOSS?

The importance of the delicate balance parents need to achieve between taking it easy and enforcing strict limits cannot be overstated. Your kids need to know that you're the boss. If you let your toddler, tween, or teenager rule your life, you will find yourself in the lowest circles of hell. A toddler just doesn't have the frontal brain development to make reasonable life choices. One time my toddler threw a tantrum because I stopped him from eating his sister's sock while it was still on her foot. He wailed, "I need eat Audrey's sock!" This is perfectly predictable behavior for a two-year-old, which indicates that you should strongly resist letting your toddler rule your world. Whether you're dealing with a toddler, tween, or a teenager, you need to be in charge.

However, the power you claim is not an iron-clad, rigid rule. The power that flexible-thinking parents can claim is to create their own reality. As a parent, you are given the power to create your own family culture. This may mean you enforce strict sleep times because you think it's fundamental to your child's well-being and your own. Your laid-back attitude might take the form of not worrying about your child smearing oatmeal on the couch. You're strict about nap times, but lax about upholding the integrity of your worldly possessions (as long as the behavior is not outright destructive). You don't have to follow anyone else's model. You have the freedom, dignity, and power to honor your own deepest values.

EXPERIMENTS

Another strategy for honoring competing viewpoints is to remember the power of experiments. This means that rather than saying to your child that he is right or wrong, you demonstrate an interest in testing his worldview or honoring it for short test runs. For example, like many children, your child may say that a class at school has no meaning to the rest of his life, so why should he care? Rather than fighting him, you can experiment with dropping the tug-of-war rope, giving him a chance to elaborate in great detail about what he imagines the rest of his life will be like and why this class is irrelevant. You don't have to buy his argument, but listen closely and show that you have heard what he said.

ACTIVITIES

The twenty-one activities you will find in the rest of this chapter will help you bridge the gap between your world and your child's world. The activities will help you establish the balance of honoring your child while maintaining your authority.

1. Finding Cool

It's important for your child to both develop self-reliance and to figure out how to be cool. Your child needs to have the inner strength to be "above the influence," as one recent antidrug campaign says. At the same time, he needs to fit in. Sometimes parents make the mistake of thinking that their child's quest to be cool is a waste of time. While the hierarchies in schools are usually incredibly superficial, it is important for your child to figure out what's cool, what's not, and play the game to some extent. The idea isn't for him to mindlessly follow what's cool, but rather to know what it is at his school. Sometimes the recipe for coolness is to know what is cool and play the game but show that you can still make up your own mind. Kids who are seen as uncool can be those who are clueless about what's cool and also those who try too hard to be cool.

For this activity, you and your child will investigate and discuss what is cool. As a parent, you will take a different approach than you might usually take. Parents fall into the mistake of either feeling disappointed that their child is not cool and conveying that displeasure in subtle ways or pooh-poohing the social wrangling as if it's irrelevant. Although these sort of ranking systems are highly superficial, they can have a great impact on your child's happiness. Ask your child the following questions and develop your own. Discuss the answers, and if you don't know the answers, create a plan for investigating (ask other parents, observe other kids at school, and so on). Here are the questions:

- What are the cool shoes for kids to wear?
- What TV shows do all the kids talk about?
- What video games do all the kids play?
- What activities and/or sports are cool?

2. Driving Activity: Creating Cool

When you are driving in the car, you can use the free time to discuss the results of the Finding Cool activity. For this discussion you can remind your child that being cool means knowing what's cool and being able to play the game but also showing the self-possession to have your own ideas. Once you know what cool is, you can make a choice and sometimes create what's cool by doing something different with it.

Share with your child stories from your own childhood and observations you have made throughout your life of people who were cool and those who were not. You may also want to talk about how being cool in school relates to the real world. This will help your child put into perspective the struggles for popularity in school. Recently,

I observed a geeky looking teen girl talking with an attractive young man working at a coffee shop. She had gone off to an impressive college while he stayed in town and worked while attending a junior college. From their conversation, it seemed likely that he had been the cool one in high school and she was probably not. While I waited to get my coffee, I realized that I was witnessing a provocative drama of tables turning: the geek—now poised to set the world on fire—talking to the cool guy who paid little attention to her in high school. Almost every adult can tell a similar story of their own friends or observations of others as they progressed through life. Share some of these stories with your child, reflecting on what it takes to be cool while also making the choices that will serve you after you get out of the short-lived but often painful years of social struggles in school.

3. Cool Screening

After having the "cool" discussion, plan an activity where both you and your child engage in one of the discoveries. You may want to watch a TV show, go to a cool movie, shop at a store with popular fashions, or attend an activity that other kids talk about. Take the opportunity to discuss how this cool stuff fits in or doesn't fit in with your family. For example, once you know what the cool TV shows are, you can allow your child to watch one of these shows, but be involved and ready to discuss the values and ideas in the show. Plan a time to watch the show together and discuss it with your child. Talk about what part of the show you want your child to learn from and what part of it you think he should reject. As an illustration, for older children, it's likely that popular shows involve sexuality in ways that no parent would want their kids to look to as a model. You can discuss with your child that while popular culture tends to flaunt sexuality, your values as a family are very different. You might be prepared with a discussion of what you think is a healthy definition or approach to sexuality.

Some parents may be concerned that if they expose their kids to activities that they don't like or have objections to, they will expose their kids to negative influences. In fact, you can think of such exposures much like a vaccine. Your children will no doubt be exposed to the ideas and values in popular shows or activities. If you interact with your child and together consider these cool things, you will have a chance to contribute your values and ideas in his process of interpreting what everyone else is doing or saying.

4. Adding and Subtracting—The Fun Kind

Part of flexible thinking is realizing that for each new thing you take into your life, you need to let go of something else. The constant increase in activity level creates stress and pressure for anyone and will make the symptoms of ADHD worse. You need to constantly monitor your child's activity level and keep it reasonable. In addition, both you and your child will need to make sure the activities you do select increase joy rather than add stress. This experiment is one you can repeat each week.

Each week select one existing activity that you and your child agree you can eliminate. At the same time, brainstorm for an activity that you can add that will increase you and your child's joy. The activity that you add should be noncompetitive and feel in alignment with your child's deepest gifts (or offer a chance to explore and find out what those gifts might be). If you struggle to find an activity to add that really packs a punch in terms of leading to excitement and joy, you and your child can make your activity a search through local magazines, surfing the Internet, and asking others for their favorite activities.

Many times we get stuck in a rut and are dragged down by habits that no longer serve any purpose, draining our energy. If you have a hard time finding an activity you can eliminate, write out a weekly schedule and review it closely with your child. As an example, you might cut out a sports activity and replace it with a family walk. You might cut out a TV show and add a family food prep night, in which everyone helps prepare some homemade treats.

5. Hide and Seek

This activity amplifies the principle of flexible thinking described in the preceding activity, honoring the yin and yang of letting go and opening to receive. In this case, you will create an activity you and your child can do where you select objects or things to get rid of and then investigate or hunt for an object or new thing to bring into the home.

You and your child can hunt around the house or his room to find the most energy-draining object. It could be a piece of art that's really an eyesore, a pile of magazines, or old sports equipment. Find something you can both agree on and throw it away, sell it on eBay or craigslist, or donate it to a charity. Then you spend some time hunting for something new to bring in that will increase energy and joy in your home or in your child's room. It might be as simple as throwing out a pile of magazines and bringing in fresh-cut flowers from your garden. It might be as complex as taking out an entertainment center in your living room and replacing it with a humble TV stand in another room to de-emphasize the centrality of TV in your home. You should repeat this activity every week.

You can also do this activity "organically" when your child asks for something new or needs something new. If you have a new purchase to make, ask your child to select one object or thing to get rid of before you bring the new thing into the home.

While this will help with the organization of your home and is an important skill for your child to gain, the main point is to demonstrate the flexible thinking of letting go and receiving. Our culture tends to emphasize the idea that more and bigger is always better. This activity and the previous one will help your child develop a thinking style that is more flexible and complex than the current culture of consumption.

6. Marshmallow Juggling

Leonardo da Vinci believed that juggling was one of the best activities for synchronizing the brain and stimulating flexible thinking. While I haven't found any scientific evidence that proves that, it's fun enough to make it worth a try.

You and your child can begin to train your minds by practicing juggling marshmallows. Buy a bag of large marshmallows and start out by trying to keep two in the air. Then move to trying to juggle three marshmallows. You might even buy a book for learning how to juggle. There are many kits that often come with a guide and some balls or scarves to begin practicing with. Scarves can be easier to start with since they fall much more slowly. After you practice juggling, you can make it even more of an event by melting some of the remaining marshmallows on a graham cracker with chocolate, making s'mores. If you and your child find this activity fun, you can make it a regular practice, building those brain connections that allow for more complex and flexible thinking.

7. Imperfection Day

As I mentioned before, one of the trickier balancing acts of parenting is how to have high standards for your child and at the same time create a healthy environment that isn't constantly tense because of unrelenting performance demands. In the arena of achievement, it's important to have high standards. In the arena of mental health, it is essential that your child not feel driven by his or his parents' needs for self-esteem. He shouldn't always feel the need to prove himself and be perfect. Perfectionism is highly correlated with depression and can become a form of self-abuse.

Your child needs to learn to have high standards but not to have undue anxiety about imperfection. One way you can keep the balance is to maintain your expectations, but eliminate harsh, unrealistic, and rigid beliefs about those expectations. (See *Listening to Depression* [Honos-Webb 2006] for a discussion of these beliefs and how to heal.) In addition, you can plan an "imperfection day" where you celebrate the human foibles and overall imperfection that none of us can escape.

You can plan this day to be one of lowered expectations, with an easygoing attitude. You could eat easy meals like sandwiches and soup rather than something complicated. You can allow for relaxation, naps, and activities that don't lead to self-improvement or fulfill performance demands.

Your child and each person in the family should honor imperfection by choosing one way to intentionally allow some form of imperfection. It may be as simple as wearing a piece of clothing that has a stain on it or a rip. You may want to find an old picture your child drew that isn't a glorious piece of artwork but is delightful in its sloppy imperfection and frame it to hang on the wall. You may choose to allow your child to wear an outfit that is messy or poorly coordinated and do the same for yourself. Find a way to express your ability to be comfortable with imperfection and laugh about it.

8. Driving Activity: Hip-Hop Hallelujahs

This activity will give you and your child a chance to practice flexibly combining seemingly incompatible worldviews into one artistic creation. It offers a chance to practice being creative and will expose him to different music without imposing your taste on him. The activity will help you and your child break out of "either/or" thinking and begin to experiment with how to combine differences and think in terms of "both/and."

This activity will bring together your kid's musical tastes and your own. You can start by selecting some of your favorite songs, playing them in the car or singing them yourself. Or you can simply give your kids your favorite lines from a song, whether it is opera, a Broadway tune, or pop music from when you were a teen.

Then you can ask your kids to take the words of this song or songs and put them to the tune of their own favorite music. For younger kids, it might be the tune of "Twinkle, Twinkle Little Star," and for older kids it might be hip-hop music or rock ballads. It's easy to imagine egging your kids on to sing the Hallelujah chorus of Handel's *Messiah* to a hip-hop beat.

You can also take turns taking words from your kids' favorite songs and singing them in the style of your favorite musical genre.

9. Read, Watch, Listen, Talk, and Draw

Select an arena that your child is intensely curious about. It may be the Amazon rain forest, a trip to Hawaii, or snowboarding. You can help foster flexible thinking by exploring this topic of intense interest in multiple domains. Go to the library and find a book, an audiotape, and a movie selection relevant to your child's area of interest. Invite your child to read the book and plan a time for you and him to listen to the audiotape together (another great driving activity) and watch the movie together. After you have explored the topic in each of those media, have a conversation about the interest and what each of you learned, what surprised you, and what was different about each of the forms of learning—reading, listening, and watching. You may want to pay attention to how your child responds to each form of media. It may give you important information in figuring out how your child learns best. Some people are saying that kids nowadays learn only through visuals because they've been exposed to too much TV. While it's true that catering to the "MTV generation" takes some thought, in general each person has a unique preference for how to take information in and learn.

After your conversation, get out some crayons, colored pencils, or any other tools for creative expression you may have and make some artwork related to the central theme you explored. By allowing your child to learn about something of great interest from so many angles, you will help him develop flexible thinking. He will also learn that he can reinforce his learning by repetition through many different channels. You can use this later if he is struggling with schoolwork, reminding him that it might help for him to write down notes about the troublesome subject or talk about it with friends or with you (a study group, of sorts). If he gets bored or frustrated with his studies, encourage him to work from another channel.

10. Healing Words

Another difficult part of parenting is training your child to be emotionally intelligent. On the one hand, you want your child to be able to feel his intense emotions and express them skillfully. On the other, you don't want to overwhelm your child with some of life's harsh realities too early. You want to protect your child and let him live a comfortable life without worrying too much. As parents, we are all too aware of possibilities for sadness or grief—grandparents can die, other important people can get sick, accidents can happen. In raising your child, you may want to keep your focus on probabilities—meaning that unless a difficult situation is likely to happen, it makes sense to protect your child from knowing about it. A child with ADHD already has so much on his plate that you might be even more inclined to protect him from other concerns.

This activity is simple: you just shower your child with reassuring comments. These will serve to allow him to relax about fears that are almost certainly lurking in his mind. Most children have heard of things like death, divorce, and sickness. Sometimes your child may be overwhelmed by his fears that one of these things could happen to his family, but he doesn't ask directly because it's too scary to even think about. So if you offer soothing statements, it might help him address anxieties he can't even talk about. Some examples of what you might say follow.

- Mommy and Daddy are healthy and happy, and we'll always be here for you.

- Mommy and Daddy love each other.
- If you have any worries, you can always talk to me.
- Don't worry alone. Tell Mommy or Daddy what you're worried about.
- We are going to keep you safe.

Remember that as long as it's likely to be true, it's okay to say it. Even though you may struggle in your marriage, it's fine to reassure your child about the relationship. But, if you know you're headed for a divorce, then you have a different challenge in finding a way to prepare your child for that.

11. Driving Activity: Thinking Inside the Box

Parents of kids with ADHD can delight in their child's creativity and yet fear the child's difficulty with paying attention to details and following rules. Creativity (one of the biggest gifts of ADHD), by definition, requires breaking existing rules or at least playing with them. Every adult knows that if you don't pay attention to details and follow the important rules, devastating results can follow. So how do you honor your child's creativity while still steering him toward the realities of succeeding in the world?

Many parents' anxiety about how their child will make it in the real, grown-up world provokes them to try to redirect their child's interests away from music, art, or photography. However, it's important to honor your child's artistic gifts while giving him some basic skills in the service of money and business management.

For this activity, you can demonstrate your respect for your child's creative passion by opening up a discussion with him about how he could earn a living with his creative expression. Egg him on to begin to think about the realities of creating a product, producing it, getting it to people who would be interested in it, taking in money, managing money, saving money, and paying taxes. You don't have to prepare your child to launch a business in current time, but as you begin to discuss the realities that he will eventually face, you will let him know that even if he does pursue a living following his creative passion, he will still have to navigate real-world complexities. If you have this "in-the-box thinking" conversation with him regularly, you are accomplishing two goals: you will improve your connection with your child while laying the groundwork for his success as an adult.

12. Wag Your Finger, Put Your Foot Down

Another tension in parenting is that you do want to connect with your child and see the world from his perspective, but at the end of the day you must be the boss. The approach in this book is meant to counteract the vicious cycle that often gets set in motion when a child is failing to live up to performance demands. The activities are meant to reestablish the connection between you and your child and help you gain a broader perspective. However, that is not meant to replace the tried-and-true tactics of parenting, including wagging your finger with stern demands such as, "No more chocolate milk" and putting your foot down, as in, "Get off that phone now."

For this activity, you will honor the other side of the coin—establishing yourself firmly as the boss. However, you can turn even that into an activity with an element of play. You can create a top ten list of rules you expect to be enforced in your home. Have a meeting with your family and share the list. With your child alone or as a family, you can create a consequence that fits with the "crime" if rules are broken. For example, rather than threatening time-outs or standard punishments, try to craft clever reinforcers like, "Whoever stays on the phone too long has to help Mom by monitoring the line when she is caught in one of those endless-loop answering services."

Each week you can create a new top-ten list, including topics like "Top Ten Ways We Treat Our Friends," "Top Ten Supportive Phrases We Use," or "Top Ten Successes We Celebrate." You can use your imagination to create a new list with your child each week to reinforce a family culture where standards are made and enforced.

13. The List

Another dilemma that parents struggle with is the desire to nourish their child's mind and spirit while not spoiling the child. Many children who are constantly stimulated struggle with the need for high levels of stimulation throughout their lives, which may create new problems. A person who needs high doses of intensity all of the time may be vulnerable to acting out, addictions, or sexual promiscuity without the capacity for intimacy, among other troubles. These problems are made worse by the constant stream of advertising almost everywhere you look. The advertising creates desires for ever-new experiences and material goods.

The other side of the dilemma is that new environments and stimulation are important to developing skills and for building intelligence and adaptability. How does a parent strike a balance between these competing demands?

One way you can respond to requests (or demands) for new toys or trips to special places is to simply say, "We'll put it on the list." In order for this to work, you have to establish a list where you record interests of your child and activities he requests to do. You can place the list in a prominent place that everyone can see at home. You can make an activity out of creating a sacred space and using art to decorate this special list.

Then, any time your child asks to participate in an activity, take a class, go to the movies, or get a new toy, game, or movie, you are not stuck coming up with a yes or a no. You can just say, "Put it on the list." With this strategy, your child can stand back and look at the way his desires pile up and how much time, energy, and money it would require to meet each impulse and want he has. This activity will help your child gain perspective on the constant stream of stimulation available to him and how he needs to be choosy about which of his desires are possible to meet.

14. Driving Activity: Greatness vs. Success

For this activity you will explore the difference with your child between greatness and success. You might be wondering what the difference is yourself. Well, you get to make up your own mind, but some guidelines might be:

- Greatness is one-of-a-kind expression with obvious contribution to the greater good.
- Success is achieving a clearly defined plan or objective, often defined by someone else.

Make up your own illustrations, examples, and samples. Then, for the activity, begin a discussion of people you know in your life or people you know about through history or current events who fall into the following categories:

- People who are great but not successful (the artist who struggles to pay the rent)
- People who are successful but not great (the embittered lawyer who sacrificed his family and true vocation for a lifestyle that conformed to others' expectations)
- People who are successful *and* great (Mother Teresa)

Use your discussion of these distinctions to reflect on important life choices that each child and parent must make. How can you balance these different demands? You and your child can discuss whether you and he value greatness or success and what choices your family and ancestors have made in the past.

15. Playing Silly Parrot and Standard Parrot

Kids with ADHD find it almost impossible to listen. This one symptom can create an avalanche of problems leading to some of the most serious impairments in functioning. A fun game you can play that gives your child a chance to build his listening skills while honoring the underlying gift is Silly Parrot and Standard Parrot. The gift underlying a failure to listen is that while he is not paying attention to words, your child is usually highly sensitive to nonverbal cues and unspoken emotions and tensions. ADHD kids may not hear a word you say, but they "have your number," so to speak. They usually can see right through you, and this distraction prevents them from actually listening to the content of what you and others are saying.

A way to honor both sides of this is to tell your child that you're going to play the Silly Parrot and Standard Parrot game. Tell him that a standard parrot listens to a person talk and then just repeats back exactly what the person has said. A silly parrot waits until the person is done speaking and then says whatever he feels like saying. Give your child the chance to play silly parrot first: 1) you say a sentence, and 2) he blurts out whatever comes to his mind. Have a good laugh together and then play standard parrot: 1) you say a sentence, and 2) he repeats it back to you exactly as you said it. You can encourage him to play each bird in a squawking "parrot" voice and ham it up. Go back and forth between the silly parrot and the standard parrot. Over time, your child will get the difference between the two styles and gain some basic skills for listening so that he can repeat things back to you as the standard parrot.

16. Going to Bat and Letting Go

Some parents fall into different camps: those who solve all their child's problems and those who let their child fend for himself. Underlying these different strategies are different core beliefs. Those who always go to bat for their child believe they have to keep their child safe from the world. Those who let their child fend for himself at every turn believe that they must let him become strong. Practicing flexible thinking means using both of these approaches strategically.

For this activity you and your child are going to work together on a creative project. You will need construction paper, crayons, markers, scissors, and magazines you can cut up. On one piece of construction paper, draw or make a collage of baseball bats. You can find some free coloring pages and relevant images at www.coloring.ws/coloring.html.

Work together to create this image, which will symbolize "going to bat" for your child. On another piece of construction paper, create a drawing or collage of barbells and images of weight lifting. This will symbolize that you need to let your child "lift weights" (handle his life struggles) to get strong. As you work on these projects, talk with your child about what these images mean for you and how he feels about these different approaches. You can create a list with your child of times when he would prefer you go to bat for him and times when he would prefer you let him go it alone. Share your view on when these different styles are appropriate. You can laminate the pictures or find frames for them and hang your artwork in the home as a reminder of finding balance between advocating for your child and letting him take responsibility.

17. Family Awards Night

For this activity you will create a family awards night where everyone gets an award and gets to make up an acceptance speech. Each person in your family should get two awards: one that reflects a personal accomplishment, something he faced and overcame pretty much alone; and one that celebrates an achievement of team-playing, or being part of a supportive environment, even if he didn't have any outstanding personal success. For example, your ADHD child might get an award for getting an A in a class that he worked really hard for and also get an award for being on a team that won a soccer game in which he didn't score a goal. Create awards for everyone in the family, and put on an Academy Awards-style event, with trophies or prizes and acceptance speeches.

This will be a fun event for the whole family and will help encourage flexible thinking about both taking responsibility for personal successes and seeing how important the environment is in what can and can't be accomplished. A successful child is optimistic because he takes credit for personal accomplishments. At the same time, a successful child has the ability to see the role the environment plays and know when he needs the support of others. The ability to look for both of these causes will help your child find the right balance of self-esteem and personal accountability. When he sees how his and his family's awards reflect both of these dimensions, he will build skills in looking for both inner and outer causal factors.

18. Dinnertime Game

Another paradox for parents to handle is the tension between the power of labels to create self-fulfilling prophecies coupled with the relief that kids and parents can feel at finding a label for the very real differences that do describe your child—the label of ADHD. As a fun way to explore this tension without necessarily resolving it, you can play the following game at dinnertime to spark lively conversation on this matter.

Create a label for every person in your family at dinner, using a mailing sticker or a small piece of paper with tape. Labels can include: Expert, Clown, Celebrity, Pushover, Tough Guy, and any others you can think of. Stick the labels on the forehead of each person at dinner without letting them see what it says. Tell the family that they cannot see their own label, but for this meal they have to treat each other person as that person's label. For example, you would laugh at whatever the Clown says or look entertained by whatever he does. At the end of the meal, ask each person to guess what the label on their forehead says.

This can be a silly and experimental way to explore the power of labels. You will probably find that each person can do a pretty good job of guessing what their label says. It will also give each person the experience of how his inner experience is powerfully impacted by the way he is being treated by others and the expectations others have for him. Spend time with your family discussing what this means on a larger scale.

19. As the World Turns

As a parent, you want to help your child learn to tolerate frustration at the same time you want to help him stay positive. This activity will help achieve this delicate balance. Get a large piece of posterboard, and along one side write the numbers from 1 to your child's current age. At each age, write the following sentence and fill in the blanks:

"At age ______, Stan could ____________________, but he couldn't __________________ yet."

You may want to complete the posterboard by yourself but share your process of filling it out with your child. As an example, you might say that "At age three, Stan could write and draw, but he couldn't spell his name yet." Then start the next age by using what he couldn't do at age three as what he *could* do at age four. Continuing the example, "At age four, Stan could spell his name, but he couldn't read yet."

Fill out the posterboard with each year of your child's life so far, showing the progression of how he mastered skills that had been out of reach the year before. If you have the time and energy, you can get creative with photos and keepsakes from the child's age pasted on the posterboard for each year. If you remember a vivid example of a time when your child got really frustrated trying to do something and can present the story in a dramatic or humorous way, that can also show your child how frustrations are part of the process of growth. The longer a child can tolerate frustration, the more likely he will persist and leap into the next challenge.

20. The Mailbox

Throughout the book, you have learned activities for fostering emotional sensitivity and skills. It can be a challenge to teach your child to stay connected to his emotions while not being overwhelmed by them. This activity will give your child a concrete way to begin to think about feeling emotions and then letting go of them.

Create a mailbox, which can be a simple office tray that says "Mailbox" or an elaborate creative creation with sparkles, bows, and even bells and whistles. Then tell your child that this will be the place where you mail your problems away. Show your child how you can write a letter to someone who can solve your problem or to someone who caused a problem and drop it in the box. If your family is religious or spiritual you can say the mailbox goes to God, Jesus, angels, a saint, or some other holy figure. If the child has an emotion that troubles him, he can write about that emotion or draw a picture of it and then put it in the box to send away to a higher power or a real person who he imagines can help him with the problem or emotion.

Tell your child that when he puts his emotion or problem in the magic mailbox, he can just let it go for now. You can use this activity to help him problem solve without being overwhelmed by his emotions. For example, if your child's feelings were hurt by something a friend did or said, you can have the child mail these hurt feelings to that child. Then you can work with your child to imagine some things he could say to that friend that would meet his needs right now. In this way your child can learn to experience his emotions but not be driven to act on them in destructive ways.

21. Sacred Spacey Place

The toughest grind for your child with ADHD is paying close attention when he just wants to space out and dream. The need to follow directions, follow a path, listen to others, practice logical thinking, stay organized, perform, and compete are often at odds with your child's cognitive style. Your child can begin to feel more and more alone as the demands pile up and he falls short. One thing you can do to show your child that his way of thinking and being is highly valued is to create a sacred spacey place. This will be an area in his room, elsewhere in the home, the garage, or even outdoors where he can create a zone to space out, daydream, and follow his inner whims. If he likes to draw, you can include drawing tools and paper in this special space. It can be a play tent that you can purchase at Wal-Mart or Target. It can be a chair with some colorful scarves hanging over the area. It could be an old futon, a sofa to be discarded, or any other soft landing that signals a cozy, comfy space-out time.

This activity, while demonstrating respect for your child's style, can also help him learn how to tell the difference between spacey daydream time and homework time or practice time. If he has a special space in which to be spacey, he'll quickly learn the difference and know how to stay in control and move from spacey to focused. In addition, when the impulse to daydream comes on strong, he can tell himself, "I can wait a few minutes and when I finish this, I'll go to my spacey place." The simple act of creating a literal space for your child's spaciness can both help him to express the gifts of spaciness and limit them at the same time.

Final Summary

If there is only one thing you take away from this book, I hope it will be to keep asking yourself, "What is right with my child?" As a parent myself, I know how your loving devotion to your children is the most demanding and most unrecognized, unappreciated work in the world. It is also, I firmly believe, the most important work in the world. The activities in this book are meant to give you some ideas for how to spend your precious time with your kids. I tried to make it so that the activities didn't require any more of your time running around trying to find pipe cleaners or clean out old milk containers, and I didn't want to bore you to tears with yet another brain-building activity.

It is a constant challenge to stay connected to your child while keeping yourself alive and interested. Too many parents tell me that they feel like they are watching the clock when playing with their children. You can create your own activities by noting what your child enjoys that also keeps you feeling alive and genuinely engaged. If you find yourself watching the clock, limit the activity to five minutes and then change it so that it meets your own needs. Many parents believe that parenting necessarily involves self-sacrifice. I hope this book will show you that parenting can be a springboard to creating the aliveness and passion for yourself and your family that you have been seeking.

Learn More About Lara Honos-Webb's Work

Explore other books, learning programs, seminars, and professional training to reinforce and advance what you've learned in this book. More details can be found at www.visionarysoul.com.

SEMINARS AND TRAINING

Dr. Lara Honos-Webb provides world-class training programs for organizations, hospitals, health care providers, and individuals.

A sample of workshop and seminar training titles includes:

- The Gift of ADHD
- Listening to Depression: How Understanding Your Pain Can Heal Your Life
- Parenting with Passion: Do What You Love, the Kids Will Follow
- Marriage Minders: A Revolutionary New Approach to Preventing Marital Blowouts
- Translate Your Pain into Purpose: An Alternative Mental Health Revolution
- Points on the Board, Oil Changes, and Tune-Ups: Getting Your Hubby to Sign On to Marital Bliss on His Own Terms
- What's Right with My Child?
- How to Deal with Challenging Behavior in Your Child
- ADHD in the Workplace
- Depression in the Workplace
- Create Emotional Intelligence in the Workplace

BOOKS AND E-BOOKS

Books

Honos-Webb, L. In press. *The Gift of Adult ADD: How to Transform Your Problems into Strengths*. Oakland, CA: New Harbinger Publications.

Honos-Webb, L. 2006. *Listening to Depression: How Understanding Your Pain Can Heal Your Life*. Oakland, CA: New Harbinger Publications.

Honos-Webb, L. 2005. *The Gift of ADHD: How to Transform Your Child's Problems into Strengths*. Oakland, CA: New Harbinger Publications.

e-Books

When Self-Help Hurts: Letting Go of Seeking by Finding Yourself. This powerful e-book will help you begin finding, rather than seeking. The simple pursuit of transformation has the effect of making you a seeker. The creation of your destiny is playful art. Its grandeur will be found in its breathtaking originality—not in its technical perfection beaten into shape through years of reform school. Available at www.visionarysoul.com.

Learning the Art of Giving Yourself Permission. This e-book reviews the healing power of giving yourself permission rather than giving yourself more demands for reform. Transform your romantic and professional life and increase your capacity to let go and have fun by practicing giving yourself permission. Available at www.visionarysoul.com.

Parenting with Passion: Do What You Love, the Children Will Follow. Parents don't have to give up on what they love, even when raising young children. This e-book will show you how to find and follow your bliss while giving your kids everything they need and more. Available at www.visionarysoul.com.

The Psychology of Pregnancy and Birth. This e-book reveals the dramatic life changes women experience during pregnancy and prepares them for birth and transition to motherhood. Available at www.visionarysoul.com.

References

Bennett, S., and N. Kalish. 2006. *The Case Against Homework*. New York: Crown.

Burnett, F. H. 2002. *The Secret Garden*. New York: Gramercy.

Dwoskin, H., and J. Canfield. 2003. *The Sedona Method: Your Key to Lasting Happiness, Success, Peace and Emotional Well-Being*. Sedona, AZ: Sedona Press.

Friedman, T. L. 2006. *The World Is Flat: A Brief History of the Twenty-first Century*. New York: Farrar, Straus and Giroux.

Gardner, H. 1999. *Intelligence Reframed: Multiple Intelligences for the 21st Century*. New York: Basic Books.

Giltay, E., M. Kamphuis, S. Kalmijn, F. Zitman, and D. Kromhout. 2006. Dispositional optimism and the risk of cardiovascular death. *Archives of Internal Medicine* 166:431-436.

Gottman, J., J. Murray, C. Swanson, R. Tyson, and K. Swanson. 2002. *The Mathematics of Marriage*. Cambridge, MA: MIT Press.

Honos-Webb, L. 2005. *The Gift of ADHD: How to Transform Your Child's Problems into Strengths*. Oakland, CA: New Harbinger Publications.

Honos-Webb, L. 2006. *Listening to Depression: How Understanding Your Pain Can Heal Your Life*. Oakland, CA: New Harbinger Publications.

Langer, E. J. 1989. *Mindfulness*. Reading, MA: Addison-Wesley

Martin, J. K., B. A. Pescosolido, S. Olafsdottir, and J. D. McLeod. 2007. The construction of fear: Americans' preferences for social distance from children and adolescents with mental health problems. *Journal of Health and Social Behavior* 48:50-67.

Paolini, C. 2004. *Eragon*. New York: Knopf.

Pink, D. H. 2005. *A Whole New Mind*. New York: Penguin.

Robbins, A. 1991. *Awaken the Giant Within*. New York: Simon & Schuster.

Rosenthal, R. 1987. Pygmalion effects: Existence, magnitude, and social importance. *Educational Researcher* 16:37-41.

Shapiro, L. E. 1997. *How to Raise a Child with a High EQ: A Parents' Guide to Emotional Intelligence*. New York: HarperCollins.

Sinetar, M. 2000. *Sometimes Enough Is Enough: Finding Spiritual Comfort in a Material World*. New York: HarperCollins.

Tarrant, J. 1998. *The Light inside the Dark: Zen, Soul and the Spiritual Life*. New York: HarperCollins.

Taylor, A. F., F. E. Kuo, and W. C. Sullivan. 2001. Coping with ADD: The surprising connection to green play settings. *Environment and Behavior* 33:54-77.

Wallis, C., and S. Steptoe. 2006. How to bring our schools out of the 20th century. *Time*, December 18 51-56.

Lara Honos-Webb, Ph.D., is a clinical psychologist licensed in California. She is author of *The Gift of ADHD* and *Listening to Depression*, which was selected by *Health Magazine* as one of the best therapy books of 2006. She is also author of the forthcoming *Gift of Adult ADD*. Her work has been featured in *Newsweek*, the *Wall Street Journal*, the *Chicago Tribune*, and *Publisher's Weekly* as well as newspapers across the country and local and national radio and television. She specializes in the treatment of ADHD and depression and the psychology of pregnancy and motherhood; she speaks regularly on her areas of expertise. Honos-Webb completed a two-year postdoctoral research fellowship at University of California, San Francisco, and has been an assistant professor teaching graduate students. She has published more than twenty-five scholarly articles. Visit her website at www.visionarysoul.com.